HEURISTIC
RESEARCH

Dedicated to:
John, Shannon, and Taryn
Sacha and Misha
Derek
and
Tyson and Brian

from whom I have learned about nature, passion,
and essence in first-person exclamations and
portrayals of what life experience is and means.

HEURISTIC RESEARCH

Design, Methodology, and Applications

CLARK MOUSTAKAS

SAGE PUBLICATIONS
The International Professional Publishers
Newbury Park   London   New Delhi

For information address:

SAGE Publications, Inc.
2111 West Hillcrest Drive
Newbury Park, California 91320

SAGE Publications Ltd.
28 Banner Street
London EC1Y 8QE
England

SAGE Publications India Pvt. Ltd.
M-32 Market
Greater Kailash I
New Delhi 110 048 India

Printed in the United States of America

Library of Congress Cataloging-in-Publication Data

Moustakas, Clark E.
    Heuristic research : design, methodology, and applications / by
Clark Moustakas.
        p.   cm.
    Includes bibliographical references.
    ISBN 0-8039-3881-0. -- ISBN 0-8039-3882-9 (pbk.)
    1. Heuristic.   2. Problem solving--Psychological aspects.
I. Title.
BD260.M68   1990
001.4'2--dc20   90-34596
                                                                     CIP

FIRST PRINTING, 1990

Sage Production Editor: Diane S. Foster

Contents

Acknowledgments

Many people contributed to the development of *Heuristic Research,* first and foremost the doctoral students who studied with me at the Merrill-Palmer Institute and Saybrook Institute following publication of my loneliness studies beginning in 1961, and since 1980 at the Center for Humanistic Studies and Union Institute. Although in this book I have directly utilized the work of only recent doctoral graduates, every year since 1961 I have made elaborations and refinements in theory, concepts, processes, methods, and applications of heuristic research, often inspired by student questions and investigations. The examples and references that appear in *Heuristic Research* represent applications of heuristic design and methodology to research and to psychotherapy.

I express my appreciation to the following persons for the borrowed excerpts from dissertations and unpublished papers that have been incorporated in various sections of *Heuristic Research*: Gayle Beck, Diane Blau, Valorie Cheyne, Jon Clark, Rick Copen, Erik Craig, Stephanie Hawka, Marion MacIntyre, Louise Malefyte, Colleen McNally, Ron Marshall, Mena Potts, Claude Prefontaine, Alfonso Rodriguez, Patricia Rourke, Dorothy Schultz, Robert Shaw, Joan Snyder, Robert Snyder, John Varani, and Lynn Vaughn. I also have derived clarifications of heuristic theory and methodology from my work with Bruce Douglass whom I acknowledge and thank.

I recognize, too, the many theorists, research investigators, and psychotherapists who contributed to my knowledge and understanding of root and poetic meanings in heuristic discovery and who are often cited and quoted in this book. This group includes Carl Rogers, whose theories and conceptual papers have encouraged, supported, and often guided my thinking; Abraham Maslow, whose investigations of self-actualizing people launched an entirely new realm of scientific study of human experience; Paul Bridgman, who emphasized personal and subjective knowledge as essential components of objectivity; Martin Buber and Sydney Jourard, who presented important conceptual refinements of heuristics in concepts of I-Thou, mutuality, mystery, and self-disclosure; and Michael Polanyi, whose philosophy and scientific journeys gave heuristic ideology added significance in concepts of tacit dimension, indwelling, and intuition, as well as particular understanding of validity in qualitative investigations.

Willard Frick contributed important understandings of the symbolic growth experience and its relationship to corrective and enhancing functions of identity and selfhood. Michael Patton elucidated the nature and significance of qualitative methodology—conceptually and in practical applications. Eugene Gendlin developed focusing processes and methods that I have utilized both in research and in psychotherapy to identify and explicate central feelings and core meanings in significant human experiences. Richard van Dusen, Maureen O'Hara, Phillip Barrineau, and Jerold Bozarth contributed to my knowledge of the important ties in theory, value, and methodology between person-centered therapy, the internal frame of reference, and heuristic inquiry.

I also thank the individuals who reviewed and assessed the manuscript and offered suggestions for elaboration, clarification, and illustration that were utilized in finalizing *Heuristic Research*. This group includes Mike Arons, Eric Craig, Willard Frick, Kevin MacNeil, and Michael Patton. The inspiration, and in many ways provocation, for developing *Heuristic Research* came from Michael Patton. Deepening of philosophic thought and distinctions between phenomenology and heuristics were provided by Mike Arons. Erik Craig was helpful in his detailed work on the manuscript and in his concrete suggestions for enhancing its organization and clarity.

From the beginning of my studies of the individual, the writings of Soren Kierkegaard, Edmund Husserl, and Gordon Allport have extended and encouraged my understanding and involvement in heuristic theory and methodology.

I express my gratitude to Vange Puszcz and Helen Saxton, who not only typed the manuscript several times but lived through it with me. I also thank Betty Moustakas, who helped create a loving and peaceful setting in which the work could establish its roots and grow. Finally, I recognize the Center for Humanistic Studies and The Union Institute which provide resources, opportunities, and support for investigations of human science research that utilizes heuristic processes and discoveries, and encouragement that has enabled subjective and objective fantasies and realities to unite and find necessary and essential value in science, psychotherapy, and everyday human experience.

Clark Moustakas

1

Introduction: Resources and Inspirations

"Heuristic" research came into my life when I was searching for a word that would meaningfully encompass the processes that I believed to be essential in investigations of human experience. The root meaning of *heuristic* comes from the Greek word *heuriskein*, meaning to discover or to find. It refers to a process of internal search through which one discovers the nature and meaning of experience and develops methods and procedures for further investigation and analysis. The self of the researcher is present throughout the process and, while understanding the phenomenon with increasing depth, the researcher also experiences growing self-awareness and self-knowledge. Heuristic processes incorporate creative self-processes and self-discoveries.

The cousin word of heuristics is *eureka*, exemplified by the Greek mathematician Archimedes' discovery of a principle of buoyancy. While taking a bath, he experienced a sudden, striking realization—the "aha" phenomenon—and ran naked through the streets shouting "eureka!" The process of discovery leads investigators to new images and meanings regarding human phenomena, but also to realizations relevant to their own experiences and lives.

As an organized and systematic form for investigating human experience, heuristic research was launched with the publication of *Loneliness* (Moustakas, 1961) and continued in my explorations of *Loneliness and Love* (Moustakas, 1972) and *The Touch of Loneliness* (Moustakas, 1975). Other works influencing the development of heuristic methodology included Maslow's (1956, 1966, 1971) research on self-actualizing persons and Jourard's (1968, 1971) investigations of self-disclosure. Also of significance in the evolution of heuristic concepts are Polanyi's elucidations of the tacit dimension (Polanyi, 1964, 1966, 1969), indwelling and personal knowledge (Polanyi, 1962); Buber's (1958, 1961, 1965) explorations of dialogue and mutuality; Bridgman's

(1950) delineations of subjective-objective truth; and Gendlin's (1962) analysis of meaning of experiencing. Rogers' work on human science (Coulson & Rogers, 1968; Rogers, 1969, 1985) added theoretical and conceptual depth to the heuristic paradigm presented in *Individuality and Encounter* (Moustakas, 1968) and *Rhythms, Rituals, and Relationships* (Moustakas, 1981). Phenomenological underpinnings of heuristics were developed in *Phenomenology, Science, and Psychotherapy* (Moustakas, 1988).

As part of my own heuristic process in creating this work, I gathered before me the relatively recent investigations for which I served as research guide. These included the inner world of teaching (Craig, 1978); transforming self-doubt into self-confidence (Prefontaine, 1979); shyness (MacIntyre, 1983); self-reclamation (Schultz, 1983); being sensitive (McNally, 1982); being inspired (Rourke, 1984); return to Mexican-American ethnic identity (Rodriguez, 1985); the mystery of everyday life (Varani, 1985); feeling unconditionally loved (Hawka, 1986); the psychologically androgynous male (Clark, 1988); synchronicity (Marshall, 1987); feeling connected to nature (J. Snyder, 1989); growing up in a fatherless home (Cheyne, 1989); rejecting love (R. Snyder, 1988); precognitive dreams (M. Potts, 1988); interaction rhythms in intimate relations (Shaw, 1989); and the experience of writing poetry (Vaughn, 1989).

Along with the above works, I brought together my personal notes and spontaneous self-reflective writings for study and analysis. I also reviewed heuristic literature and reexamined my seminar outlines and presentations on heuristic design and methodology. I returned to lyric poetry, autobiography, and biography. I engaged in an immersion process, open and receptive to the nature of discovery, welcoming alternating rhythms of concentrated focus and inventive distraction. I searched within my knowledge and experience for deepened and extended awareness that would further illuminate structures and essences of heuristic discovery. I found particular meaning in studies that exemplified the heuristic paradigm and provided practical methods and procedures for its operational effectiveness in investigating human experience.

The heuristic process is a way of being informed, a way of knowing. Whatever presents itself in the consciousness of the investigator as perception, sense, intuition, or knowledge represents an invitation for further elucidation. What appears, what shows itself as itself, casts a light that enables one to come to know more fully what something is and means. In such a process not only is knowledge extended but the self of the researcher is illuminated. Descartes' assertion accurately describes the perspective of the heuristic researcher: No one can convince me "that I am nothing as long as I think myself to be something . . . I *am*, I *exist*, every time it is pronounced by me, or mentally conceived, it necessarily is true," (Descartes, 1977).

From the beginning and throughout an investigation, heuristic research involves self-search, self-dialogue, and self-discovery; the research question and the methodology flow out of inner awareness, meaning, and inspiration. When I consider an issue, problem, or question, I enter into it fully. I focus on it with unwavering attention and interest. I search introspectively, meditatively, and reflectively into its nature and meaning. My primary task is to recognize whatever exists in my consciousness as a fundamental awareness, to receive and accept it, and then to dwell on its nature and possible meanings. With full and unqualified interest, I am determined to extend my understanding and knowledge of an experience. I begin the heuristic investigation with my own self-awareness and explicate that awareness with reference to a question or problem until an essential insight is achieved, one that will throw a beginning light onto a critical human experience.

In the process of a heuristic search, I may challenge, confront, or even doubt my understanding of a human concern or issue; but when I persist in a disciplined and devoted way I ultimately deepen my knowledge of the phenomenon. In the heuristic process, I am personally involved. I am searching for qualities, conditions, and relationships that underlie a fundamental question, issue, or concern.

In heuristic investigations, I may be entranced by visions, images, and dreams that connect me to my quest. I may come into touch with new regions of myself, and discover revealing connections with others. Through the guides of a heuristic design, I am able to see and understand in a different way.

If I am investigating the meaning of delight, then delight hovers nearby and follows me around. It takes me fully into its confidence and I take it into mine. Delight becomes a lingering presence; for awhile, there is only delight. It opens me to the world in a joyous way and takes me into a richness, playfulness and childlikeness that move freely and effortlessly. I am ready to see, feel, touch, or hear whatever opens me to a fuller knowledge and understanding of the experience of delight.

In heuristics, an unshakable connection exists between what is out there, in its appearance and reality, and what is within me in reflective thought, feeling, and awareness. It is I the person living in a world with others, alone yet inseparable from the community of others; I who see and understand something, freshly, as if for the first time; I who come to know essential meanings inherent in my experience. I stand out within my experiences and in the entire domain of my interest and concern. Moffitt (1971, p. 149) captures this kind of seeing and knowing in his poem "To Look At Any Thing":

> To look at any thing
> If you would know that thing,
> You must look at it long:
> To look at this green and say
> "I have seen spring in these
> Woods," will not do—you must
> Be the thing you see:
> You must be the dark snakes of
> Stems and ferny plumes of leaves,
> You must enter in
> To the small silences between
> The leaves,
> You must take your time
> And touch the very place
> They issue from.

In Moffitt's sense, as a researcher I am the person who is challenged to apprehend the meaning of things and to give these meanings ongoing life. I provide the light that guides the explication of something and knowledge of it. When I illuminate a question, it comes to life. When I understand its constituents, it emerges as something solid and real.

Emphasis on the investigator's internal frame of reference, self-searching, intuition, and indwelling lies at the heart of heuristic inquiry. An example of the opening of a heuristic search may be found in Roads' *Talking With Nature* (1987).

Before anything else could become part of his knowledge, Roads entered into a dialogue with trees, plants, animals, birds, and the earth. He heard nature speak to him, "Help yourself. If you wish to tell the story of our connection, then write from the point of contact which you are" (p. 1). Roads responded: "How can we write of unseen realities, hint of unheard concepts, or even demonstrate the practicality of inner truths, without disturbing the slumbering Self within?" (p. 22). The answer: "Let go and fall into the river. Let the river of life sweep you beyond all aid from old and worn concepts. I will support you. Trust me. As you swim from an old consciousness, blind to higher realities beyond your physical world, trust that I will guide you with care and love into a new stream of consciousness. I will open a new world before you. Can you trust me enough to let go of the known and swim in an unknown current?" (p. 26).

It is just this swimming into an "unknown current" that is so striking in heuristic beginnings. The dawning of awareness may be refreshing and peaceful, or it may be disturbing and even jarring. Whatever the effect, the heuristic process requires a return to the self, a recognition of self-awareness, and a valuing of one's own experience. The heuristic process challenges me to rely on my own resources, and to gather within myself the full scope of my observations, thoughts, feelings, senses, and intuitions; to accept as authentic and valid whatever will open new channels for clarifying a topic, question, problem, or puzzlement.

I begin the heuristic journey with something that has called to me from within my life experience, something to which I have associations and fleeting awarenesses but whose nature is largely unknown. In such an odyssey, I know little of the territory through which I must travel. But one thing is certain, the mystery summons me and lures me "to let go of the known and swim in an unknown current."

Essentially, in the heuristic process, I am creating a story that portrays the qualities, meanings, and essences of universally unique experiences. Through an unwavering and steady inward gaze and inner freedom to explore and accept *what is,* I am reaching into deeper and deeper regions of a human problem or experience and coming to know and understand its underlying dynamics and constituents more and more fully. The initial "data" is within me; the challenge is to discover and explicate its nature. In the process, I am not only lifting out the essential meanings of an experience, but I am actively awakening and transforming my own self. Self-understanding and self-growth occur simultaneously in heuristic discovery. Buber (1961) has brought to life the heuristic power of telling a story in the right way and the concurrent shift in one's life and being. The story of a crucial human experience must be told in such a way that in itself it enables self-transformation, as in Buber's tale of the lame grandfather who, while imitating the way in which his holy Baal Shem would hop and dance while praying, suddenly himself began to hop and dance and was dramatically cured of his lameness.

To capture the resources and powers of telling one's story, one engages the full range of self-resources. One draws out all that is present in context and content in an active and lively unfolding drama, and brings one's knowledge and experience into poetical depictions. Heuristic research is a demanding process. It requires "rigorous definition, careful collection of data, and a thorough and disciplined analysis. It places immense responsibility on the researcher." (Frick, 1990, p. 79). In heuristic research the investigator must have had a direct, personal encounter with the phenomenon being investigated. There must have been actual autobiographical connections. ✓ Unlike phenomenological studies in which the researcher need not have had the experience (e.g., giving birth through artificial insemination), the heuristic researcher has undergone the experience in a vital, intense, and full way—if not the experience as such, then a comparable or equivalent experience. For example, Nancy Bernthal (1990) studied the experience of first-time parenthood with an adopted foreign child. Bernthal investigated the topic using heuristic methodology, on the basis of first-time parenthood of her own "natural birth" child.

The heuristic research process is not one that can be hurried or timed by the clock or calendar. It demands the total presence, honesty, maturity, and integrity of a researcher who not only strongly desires to know and understand but is willing to commit endless hours of sustained immersion and focused concentration on one central question, to risk the opening of wounds and passionate concerns, and to undergo the personal transformation that exists as a possibility in every heuristic journey.

TIME

Direct personal Exc

Rely on own Res.

Essential mean

NO STRICT

2

Heuristic Concepts, Processes, and Validation

Heuristic inquiry is a process that begins with a question or problem which the researcher seeks to illuminate or answer. The question is one that has been a personal challenge and puzzlement in the search to understand one's self and the world in which one lives. The heuristic process is autobiographic, yet with virtually every question that matters personally there is also a social—and perhaps universal—significance.

Heuristics is a way of engaging in scientific search through methods and processes aimed at discovery; a way of self-inquiry and dialogue with others aimed at finding the underlying meanings of important human experiences. The deepest currents of meaning and knowledge take place within the individual through one's senses, perceptions, beliefs, and judgments. This requires a passionate, disciplined commitment to remain with a question intensely and continuously until it is illuminated or answered.

CONCEPTS AND PROCESSES OF HEURISTIC RESEARCH

Identifying with the Focus of Inquiry

Through exploratory open-ended inquiry, self-directed search, and immersion in active experience, one is able to get inside the question, become one with it, and thus achieve an understanding of it. Salk (1983) has called this kind of identification with the focus of the investigation "the inverted perspective" and has described the process as follows:

In order to understand what follows it will be necessary for me to refer
to certain effects of inverted perspective which I have found valuable in
my scientific work and which I have also used as a device to understand
the human condition. I do not remember exactly at what point I began to
apply this way of examining my experience, but very early in my life I
would imagine myself in the position of the object in which I was
interested. Later, when I became a scientist, I would picture myself as a
virus, or as a cancer cell, for example, and try to sense what it would be
like to be either. I would also imagine myself as the immune system, and
I would try to reconstruct what I would do as an immune system engaged
in combating a virus or cancer cell . . . Before long, this internal dialogue
became second nature to me; I found that my mind worked this way all
the time. (p. 7)

Self-Dialogue   *to EMBRACE "IT"*

In addition to the significance of becoming one with what one is
seeking to know, one may enter into dialogue with the phenomenon,
allowing the phenomenon to speak directly to one's own experience,
to be questioned by it. In this way, one is able to encounter and
examine it, to engage in a rhythmic flow with it—back and forth, again
and again—until one has uncovered its multiple meanings. Then one
is able to depict the experience in its many aspects or foldings into
core themes and essences. Self-dialogue is the critical beginning; the
recognition that if one is going to be able to discover the constituents
and qualities that make up an experience, one must begin with
oneself. One's own self-discoveries, awarenesses, and
understandings are the initial steps of the process.

Heuristic inquiry requires that one be open, receptive, and attuned
to all facets of one's experience of a phenomenon, allowing comprehension and compassion to mingle and recognizing the place and
unity of intellect, emotion, and spirit. The heuristic researcher is
seeking to understand the wholeness and the unique patterns of
experiences in a scientifically organized and disciplined way. Heuristics, like any other science, is "a search for unity in hidden likenesses"
(Bronowski, 1965, p. 13). Craig (1978) has emphasized that in scientific
inquiry the heuristic process moves from whole to part and back to
whole again, "from the individual to the general and back again . . .
from the feeling to the word and back to the feeling, from the experience to the concept and back to the experience" (p. 57).

Gestalt

Rogers (1969) has summarized the essential qualities of discovery in terms of openness to one's own experiences, trust in one's self-awareness and understanding, an internal locus of evaluation, and a willingness to enter into a process rooted in the self. Preliminary awareness of one's own knowledge and experience of a critical life issue, challenge, or problem enables one to begin a study of the problem or concern. As the inquiry expands, such self-knowledge enables one to develop the ability and skill to understand the problem more fully, and ultimately to deepen and extend the understanding through the eyes and voices of others. Maslow (1966) has emphasized that "there is no substitute for experience, none at all. All the other paraphernalia of communication and of knowledge—words, labels, concepts, symbols, theories, formulas, sciences—all are useful only because people already knew them experientially" (pp. 45-46).

The process of self-dialogue makes possible the derivation of a body of scientific knowledge that is useful. Such a process is guided by a conception that knowledge grows out of direct human experience and can be discovered and explicated initially through self-inquiry.

In their reflections on human inquiry, Douglass and Moustakas (1985) have observed that

> learning that proceeds heuristically has a path of its own. It is self-directed, self-motivated, and open to spontaneous shift. It defies the shackles of convention and tradition. . . . It pushes beyond the known, the expected, or the merely possible. Without the restraining leash of formal hypotheses, and free from external methodological structures that limit awareness or channel it, the one who searches heuristically may draw upon the perceptual powers afforded by . . . direct experience. (p. 44)

In self-dialogue, one faces oneself and must be honest with oneself and one's experience relevant to the question or problem. Jourard (1971) has pointed out that self-disclosure is "the act of making yourself manifest, showing yourself so others can perceive you" (p. 19). Douglass and Moustakas (1985) also stress the value of self-disclosure: "At the heart of heuristics lies an emphasis on disclosing the self as a way of facilitating disclosure from others—a response to the tacit dimension within oneself sparks a similar call from others" (p. 50).

An example of self-dialogue is presented in Varani's (1985) heuristic investigation of the psychological dimensions of mystery. In the initial phase of his study, Varani maintained a journal in which he recorded dialogues with himself as a way of entering into the phenomenon of mystery. He immersed himself in the topic and clarified for himself its nature, meaning, and essence. Excerpts from his self-dialogue on the mystery of dying and death follow.

March 23, 1982

> JOHN   You sound overwhelmed under a deluge of all of these references to death and dying. Is that true?
>
> JOHN PAUL   Yes, that is true. It's like Niagara Falls crashing down upon me. The overwhelming facts about the widespread, omnipresent reality of death, offer no escape from dying. . . .
>
> JOHN   Do you have anything in particular to say about your experience of the mystery of death?
>
> JOHN PAUL   Well, I am immersed in the reality of death more often than I am aware of it or make conscious allusions to it. My guess is I could remain immersed in it; dwell in it; allow the heuristic process to move me along. I feel heavy, pressured, sad, but not depressed. I can smell death all around. Winter particularly is a time when death seems almost visible once the snow has melted and it remains still too cold for spring to come. All is dead, the trees and grass; the shrubs look beaten down; even the evergreen is pale and brown—no life at all.
>
> JOHN   Is there anyway I can assist you in this process?
>
> JOHN PAUL   Yes, I can be helped to remain in continuity with my historical personage.
>
> JOHN   How can I help here?
>
> JOHN PAUL   Jog my memory; keep before me the list of personal experiences with death.
>
> JOHN   The deaths of your mother, father, Peter, Bob Webb, stand out quite strongly, I believe. The early childhood experiences: wakes in neighbor's living rooms; the tragic deaths of family friends on Christmas Eve, writing out your will and obituary . . .
>
> JOHN PAUL   Yes, these do stand out. The failure to discuss our fears about death while growing up still smarts. I suppose being in the ministry today offered a way to deal with death . . . a step away.
>
> JOHN   What about the experience of mystery around death? Can you discuss the experience?

JOHN PAUL   I would like to. However, let me rest on it. I want to stop at
this point.

March 24, 1982

JOHN PAUL   I'm not sure I am anymore ready to focus on the experience
of death's mystery, especially my own death, than yesterday. What
comes to the surface is the unknown time when it will happen to
me. Even saying it in such a passive voice strikes me as odd and
unwanted.
JOHN   Are you saying that the time factor is mysterious, obviously
unknown? And that you will die is not a choice? This too, is
mysterious?
JOHN PAUL   Yes, both of these are. When it will be disturbs me; how it
will be, puzzles me; that I cannot choose to die at a certain time or
place, causes me to be confused. It is out of my hands, beyond my
control. Death is such an important event in my life and I am
helpless to see its execution. Uncertainty looms large about the
unknown time factor; out-of-hands aspect comes next; finally, just
"how" it will be creates some discomfort. . . .
JOHN   Since you have mentioned key themes surrounding your
experience of dying and death, could you now describe just what
is your experience with each of them? How do you relate to each
theme?
JOHN PAUL   Taking the first theme, i.e., *the uncertainty of the time of my
death,* I have tended to value time as a premium, as most precious.
Time seems to be my life itself. I don't always maintain this attitude,
yet, I would like to value time deeply on a consistent basis. This
does not mean that the here and now is lived exclusively. I value
my past and I look forward to a promising future. As I blend these
time components, I can bring an ever deeper meaning to my future
goals.
JOHN   As I hear you, the upset about the mysterious moment of
your dying can be an incentive to being vulnerable to the present
moment, an openness to what it can offer, or, in another sense, what
you can bring to it on the basis of your intentional energies, while
maintaining a sense of continuity with the past.
JOHN PAUL   You have it. . . . Moving on to the second theme that puzzles
me: *the uncontrollability issue.* As I ponder this, I sense it not as a
critical and insurmountable issue. Truly experiencing death as a
passive event bothers me. I would prefer to surrender myself at the

appropriate moment. This seems plausible and not too mysterious an event. Clearly I do not mean to take my life in suicide. For this would do violence to life's dignity for me. In another sense I am doing just that according to the truth of an old axiom: "What you sow, that is what you shall reap". My present life style, the totality of it, is moving me in the direction that will ultimately result in my death. Yet, this is not a conscious suicidal approach as it was not for Jesus or Thomas More who elected to remain true to their convictions which ultimately resulted in their executions. It seems to be the paradoxical nature of life; is it not of the essence of life to live and move towards dying? . . .

June 7, 1982

JOHN   You are saying that as you sow your life, so will you reap the harvest, death being one of the fruits. You have some control, the same as you have of determining the present use of your time and in giving your life direction.

JOHN PAUL   Yes, it is the unpredictable illness or accident for which I cannot account, that allows the mysterious unknown to associate with the uncertain aspect of life.

JOHN   Are you including in your description of the experience both uncertainty and unpredictability (i.e., of the particular circumstance)?

JOHN PAUL   Yes. It is these two themes in the mystery with which I must learn to cope. The final theme mentioned earlier, *the exact how,* seems now to be submerged in the first two themes.

Tacit Knowing

Underlying all other concepts in heuristic research, at the base of all heuristic discovery, is the power of revelation in tacit knowing. Polanyi (1983) has stated that all knowledge consists or is rooted in acts of comprehension that are made possible through tacit knowing: "*We can know more than we can tell.* . . . Take an example. We know a person's face, and can recognize it among a million. Yet we usually cannot tell how we recognize a face we know . . . this knowledge cannot be put into words" (p. 4). Such knowledge is possible through a tacit capacity that allows one to sense the unity or wholeness of something from an

understanding of the individual qualities or parts. Knowledge of the trunk, branches, buds, flowers, leaves, colors, textures, sounds, shape, size—and other parts or qualities—ultimately may enable a sense of the treeness of a tree, and its wholeness as well. This knowing of the essence or treeness of a tree is achieved through a tacit process. Vague and defined dimensions or components take on "sharp outlines of certainty, only to dissolve again in the light of second thoughts or of further experimental observations. Yet from time to time certain visions of the truth, having made their appearance, continue to gain strength both by further reflection and additional evidence," (Polanyi, 1964, p. 30).

Polanyi (1964) calls the elements of tacit knowledge *subsidiary* and *focal*. The subsidiary factors attract immediate attention; they are essential to knowing, but of secondary importance. They stand out when we examine our experience. They are the elements of perception that enter into conscious awareness. They are visible and can be described. Each time we look, we may become aware of subsidiary elements as vague shapes, outlines, or understandings that take on a definite form. Ultimately, subsidiary factors represent the invariant constituents (those which are unique and distinctive). They combine with the focal (unseen and invisible) aspects of an experience, thus making possible a sense of the wholeness or essence of a phenomenon. The focal is a necessary component in the achievement of unity or integration. Because *focal* is associated with focus, perhaps a more appropriate designation would be *implicit* or *subliminal;* nonetheless, Polanyi's language will be retained here.

In *Knowing and Being,* Polanyi (1969) considers four types of tacit knowing in which subsidiary and focal dimensions come together to create whole experiences. The first "skill" (p. 182) requires an integration of subsidiary and focal qualities such as those in learning to ride a bicycle. In this activity, a set of subsidiary skills are required, such as pedaling, steering, balancing, braking, a sense of space, timing, appropriate motions, and coordination; along with focal factors such as readiness, self-esteem, confidence, optimism, and sense of the whole—all of which are combined when riding a bicycle. When the subsidiary skills and focal attitudes are in rhythm, the person is able to fulfill the task and complete the performance.

Polanyi (1964) refers to a second type of tacit knowledge as "reading of a physiognomy" (p. 182). In understanding the mood of a person—

for example, worry—we note the furrowed brow, the downcast eyes, the lowered body, the heaviness of movement, the pinched voice and mouth, and other clues in catching the whole mood. These are the subsidiary elements. The sense of stress, heaviness, the basic inner downcast state, and other tacit signs represent the focal dimensions. Together they enable a reading of the person's state of being or mental outlook. Polanyi believes that we attend *from* the subsidiary features "*to* the mood by integrating them to the appearance of the mood" (p. 182) and that this enables us to determine the meaning of a person's outlook or prevailing attitude.

The third type of tacit knowing is involved in the way we find our way in the dark—for example, entering a theater after a movie has begun. We grope in the darkness but there are flashes of light. We "feel" our way along, picking up subsidiary clues and combining them with our sense of the focal qualities of space, shadow, and light. We develop a sense or meaning of where we are and thus are able to locate an empty seat.

Finally, Polanyi refers to "speculative skills" as tapping into the tacit dimension. For example, "a chess player conducting a game sees the way the chess-men jointly bear on his chances of winning the game" (p. 182). The chess player utilizes subsidiary and focal factors that operate in tacit knowing and is thus able to decide on the next move.

When we curtail the tacit in research, we limit possibilities for knowing. We restrict the potential for new awareness and understanding. We reduce the range and depth of meanings that are inherent in every significant human experience (Douglass & Moustakas, 1985). In obtaining information that will contribute to resolution of an issue, or illumination of a problem, the tacit dimension underlies and precedes intuition and guides the researcher into untapped directions and sources of meaning. Tacit knowing is a basic capacity of the self of the researcher and gives "birth to the hunches and vague, formless insights that characterize heuristic discovery" (Douglass & Moustakas, p. 49).

Emphasizing the indispensable nature of the tacit dimension in discovery of knowledge Polanyi (1969) asserts that: "while tacit knowledge can be possessed by itself, explicit knowledge must rely on being tacitly understood and applied. Hence all knowledge is *either tacit* or *rooted in tacit knowledge*" (p. 144).

focal → the tacit = implicit knowledge
subsidiary → the observable = explicit " "
intuition

Intuition

From the tacit dimension, a kind of bridge is formed between the implicit knowledge inherent in the tacit and the explicit knowledge which is observable and describable. The bridge between the explicit and the tacit is the realm of the between, or the intuitive. In intuition, from the subsidiary or observable factors one utilizes an internal capacity to make inferences and arrive at a knowledge of underlying structures or dynamics. Intuition makes immediate knowledge possible without the intervening steps of logic and reasoning. While the tacit is pure mystery in its focal nature—ineffable and unspecifiable—in the intuitive process one draws on clues; one senses a pattern or underlying condition that enables one to imagine and then characterize the reality, state of mind, or condition. In intuition we perceive something, observe it, and look and look again from clue to clue until we surmise the truth.

The more that intuition is exercised and tested, the more likely one will develop an advanced perceptiveness and sensitivity to what is essential in discovery of knowledge. Polanyi (1969) views the lived, expressed intuition as a skill, developed into effectiveness through practice. Referring to intuition, he states that "great powers of scientific intuition are called originality, for they discover things that are most surprising and make men see the world in a new way" (p. 118).

Intuition makes possible the perceiving of things as wholes. For example, one can view a tree from many angles, sides, front, and back; but one cannot see a whole tree. The whole tree must be intuited from the clues that are provided by careful observation, experience, and connecting the parts and subtleties of the tree into patterns and relationships that ultimately enable an intuitive knowing of the tree as a whole. Every act of achieving integration, unity, or wholeness of anything requires intuition. At every step along the way, the heuristic researcher exercises intuitive clues and make necessary shifts in method, procedure, direction, and understanding which will add depth, substance, and essential meanings to the discovery process.

Intuition is an essential characteristic of seeking knowledge. Without the intuitive capacity to form patterns, relationships, and inferences, essential material for scientific knowledge is denied or lost. Intuition facilitates the researcher's process of asking questions about phenomena that hold promise for enriching life. In substance, intuition guides the researcher in discovery of patterns and meanings that will lead to enhanced meanings, and deepened and extended knowledge.

Indwelling

Indwelling refers to the heuristic process of turning inward to seek a deeper, more extended comprehension of the nature or meaning of a quality or theme of human experience. It involves a willingness to gaze with unwavering attention and concentration into some facet of human experience in order to understand its constituent qualities and its wholeness. To understand something fully, one dwells inside the subsidiary and focal factors to draw from them every possible nuance, texture, fact, and meaning. The indwelling process is conscious and deliberate, yet it is not lineal or logical. It follows clues wherever they appear; one dwells inside them and expands their meanings and associations until a fundamental insight is achieved.

A person's anger, for example, is an experience that invites self-engagement. One becomes attuned to whatever appears in thoughts, feelings, impressions, and even glimmerings or fleeting awarenesses. In the heuristic process of indwelling one seeks to understand the nature and meaning of anger. Ultimately one seeks to apprehend anger in a living sense: its qualities, the conditions (internally and externally) that evoke it, the events, places, and people connected with it. The process of indwelling requires that one remain with one's anger and return to it again and again, until one is able to depict it fully in words and pictures, and perhaps even in creative expressions such as through poetry, artworks, movements, and narratives. Indwelling requires practice to enable the researcher to tap into intuitive awakenings and tacit mysteries as well as the explicit dimensions which can be observed, reported, and described.

Throughout a heuristic inquiry, indwelling is an essential process; particularly in the elucidation of the parameters and details of the experience. The concentrated, heavy work of heuristic research is part of the demand of the explication process, a process through which one gathers detailed life experiences related to the qualities and constituents of the phenomenon under investigation. Through the explication process, one's understanding of the phenomenon is deepened and extended. Explication requires reflective analysis, a return to the phenomenon for a more complete perspective. Indwelling is a painstaking, deliberate process. Patience and incremental understanding are the guidelines. Through indwelling, the heuristic investigator finally turns the corner and moves toward the ultimate creative synthesis that portrays the essential qualities and meanings of an experience.

Focusing

Another essential process in heuristic inquiry is that of focusing. It is both a concept that points to a significant idea relevant to personal growth, insight, and change, and a process that has been perfected and advanced as a therapeutic strategy by Gendlin (1978).   *See p. 122*

The steps of focusing as used in heuristic research include the clearing of an inward space to enable one to tap into thoughts and feelings that are essential to clarifying a question; getting a handle on the question; elucidating its constituents; making contact with core themes; and explicating the themes. Focusing facilitates a relaxed and receptive state, enables perceptions and sensings to achieve more definitive clarification, taps into the essence of what matters, and sets aside peripheral qualities or feelings.

Focusing is an inner attention, a staying with, a sustained process of systematically contacting the more central meanings of an experience. Focusing enables one to see something as it is and to make whatever shifts are necessary to remove clutter and make contact with necessary awarenesses and insights into one's experiences.

Douglass and Moustakas (1985) conclude that the focusing process enables the researcher to identify qualities of an experience that have remained out of conscious reach primarily because the individual has not paused long enough to examine his or her experience of the phenomenon. Through the focusing process, the researcher is able to determine the core themes that constitute an experience, identify and assess connecting feelings and thoughts, and achieve cognitive knowledge that includes "refinements of meaning and perception that register as internal shifts and alterations of behavior" (p. 51).

The Internal Frame of Reference

Heuristic processes relate back to the internal frame of reference. Whether the knowledge derived is attained through tacit, intuitive, or observed phenomena—whether the knowledge is deepened and extended through indwelling, focusing, self-searching, or dialogue with others—its medium or base is the internal frame of reference. To know and understand the nature, meanings, and essences of any human experience, one depends on the internal frame of reference of the person who has had, is having, or will have the experience. Only the experiencing persons—by looking at their own experiences in perceptions, thoughts, feelings, and sense—can validly provide portrayals of the experience. If one is to know and understand another's experience, one must converse directly with the person. One must encourage the other to express, explore, and explicate the meanings that are within his or her experience. One must create an atmosphere of openness and trust, and a connection with the other that will inspire that person to share his or her experience in unqualified, free, and unrestrained disclosures. Rogers (1951) has emphasized that the empathic understanding of another person's internal frame of reference is an essential condition of constructive personality change. Our most significant awarenesses are developed from our own internal searches and from our attunement and empathic understandings of others.

Our behavior will sometimes appear to be irrational when viewed from the outside, when observed from an external frame of reference. Lorenz's study of imprinting, reported in Combs, Richards, and Richards (1976), is a humorous example of how our understanding of other persons' experiences is distorted when we fail to recognize the phenomenal world of the experiencing persons, when we fail to seek to understand individuals' behavior and experiences through their perceptions and feelings and the meanings that they attach to their activities.

So it came about, on a certain Whit-Sunday, that, in company with my ducklings, I was wandering about, squatting and quacking, in a May-green meadow at the upper part of our garden. I was congratulating myself on the obedience and exactitude with which my ducklings came waddling after me, when I suddenly looked up and saw the garden fence framed by a row of dead-white faces: a group of tourists was standing at the fence and staring horrified in my direction. Forgivable! For all they could see was a big man with a beard dragging himself, crouching, round the meadow, in figures of eight, glancing constantly over his shoulder and quacking—but the ducklings, the all-revealing and all-explaining ducklings—were hidden in the tall spring grass from the view of the astonished crowd. (p. 43)

THE PHASES OF HEURISTIC RESEARCH

Six phases of heuristic research guide unfolding investigations and comprise the basic research design. They include: the initial engagement, immersion into the topic and question, incubation, illumination, explication, and culmination of the research in a creative synthesis. Each phase is discussed briefly in the sections which follow and in detailed applications in the next chapter.

Initial Engagement

Within each researcher exists a topic, theme, problem, or question that represents a critical interest and area of search. The task of the initial engagement is to discover an intense interest, a passionate concern that calls out to the researcher, one that holds important social meanings and personal, compelling implications. The initial engagement invites self-dialogue, an inner search to discover the topic and question. During this process one encounters the self, one's autobiography, and significant relationships within a social context.

Ultimately, these forces come together and form a question. The question lingers within the researcher and awaits the disciplined commitment that will reveal its underlying meanings. The engagement or encountering of a question that holds personal power is a process that requires inner receptiveness, a willingness to enter fully into the theme, and to discover from within the spectrum of life experiences that will clarify and expand knowledge of the topic and illuminate the terms of the question. During the initial engagement, the investigator reaches inward for tacit awareness and knowledge, permits intuition to run freely, and elucidates the context from which the question takes form and significance.

Immersion

Once the question is discovered and its terms defined and clarified, the researcher lives the question in waking, sleeping, and even dream states. Everything in his or her life becomes crystallized around the question. The immersion process enables the researcher to come to be on intimate terms with the question—to live it and grow in knowledge and understanding of it.

The researcher is alert to all possibilities for meaning and enters fully into life with others wherever the theme is being expressed or talked about—in public settings, in social contexts, or in professional meetings. Virtually anything connected with the question becomes raw material for immersion, for staying with, and for maintaining a sustained focus and concentration. People, places, meetings, readings, nature—all offer possibilities for understanding the phenomenon. Primary concepts for facilitating the immersion process include spontaneous self-dialogue and self-searching, pursuing intuitive clues or hunches, and drawing from the mystery and sources of energy and knowledge within the tacit dimension.

Incubation

Incubation is the process in which the researcher retreats from the intense, concentrated focus on the question. Although the researcher is moving on a totally different path, detached from involvement with the question and removed from awareness of its nature and meanings, on another level expansion of knowledge is taking place. During this process the researcher is no longer absorbed in the topic in any direct way or alert to things, situations, events, or people that will contribute to an understanding of the phenomenon. Nevertheless, growth is taking place. The period of incubation enables the inner tacit dimension to reach its full possibilities; for example, the house key that has been misplaced often evades one's recall of its location while one is totally preoccupied with finding it. Almost as soon as one is absorbed with something else, however, the key suddenly appears in consciousness and draws its owner to it. More common perhaps is the forgotten name: No matter how hard and long one concentrates on remembering, the name does not present itself. Incubating the name while being involved with something else often brings it into awareness.

A similar process occurs in heuristic inquiry. The period of incubation allows the inner workings of the tacit dimension and intuition to continue to clarify and extend understanding on levels outside the immediate awareness. Using Poincare's findings in mathematics in *Science, Faith and Society*, Polanyi (1964) asserted that discovery does not ordinarily occur through deliberate mental operations and directed calculated efforts

> the way you reach the peak of a mountain by putting in your last ounce of strength—but more often comes in a flash after a period of rest or distraction. Our labors are spent as it were in an unsuccessful scramble among the rocks and in the gullies on the flanks of the hill and then when we would give up for a moment and settle down to tea we suddenly find ourselves transported to the top . . . by a process of spontaneous mental reorganization uncontrolled by conscious effort. (p. 34)

Like Archimedes, who discovered a principle of buoyancy and displacement of fluids while taking a bath, the heuristic researcher through the incubation process gives birth to a new understanding or perspective that reveals additional qualities of the phenomenon, or a vision of its unity. Incubation is a process in which a seed has been planted; the seed undergoes silent nourishment, support, and care that produces a creative awareness of some dimension of a phenomenon or a creative integration of its parts or qualities.

Illumination

The process of illumination is one that occurs naturally when the researcher is open and receptive to tacit knowledge and intuition. The illumination as such is a breakthrough into conscious awareness of qualities and a clustering of qualities into themes inherent in the question. The illumination process may be an awakening to new constituents of the experience, thus adding new dimensions of knowledge. Or, the illumination may involve corrections of distorted understandings or disclosure of hidden meanings. When the researcher is in a receptive state of mind without conscious striving or concentration, the insight or modification occurs. A degree of reflectiveness is essential, but the mystery of situations requires tacit workings to uncover meanings and essences.

Illumination opens the door to a new awareness, a modification of an old understanding, a synthesis of fragmented knowledge, or an altogether new discovery of something that has been present for some time yet beyond immediate awareness. For example, after passing a particular scene back and forth many times I decided recently to capture its landmarks in my memory. I recorded the scene in a dated personal journal. Then I saw something that totally shocked me: On the fifth trip I was just passing—not particularly noticing anything— when a large cemetery plot suddenly appeared and caught my attention. Of course, it had been there all along, perhaps within my vision and perception, but beyond immediate attention; it was not among the core qualities that I had identified. I looked again. It was still there. I saw it distinctly and realized not only that it was a core component of the scene, but that it now virtually dominated everything else.

My original core qualities were objects of beauty in nature—fall flowers, mature trees, unusual shapes, striking greens, peaks and valleys, and brilliant colors, all burgeoning with life. What I had missed or ignored was the symbolic presence of death. Then all at once I remembered that my friend's sister had suddenly died. I had been informed at a time and place where I was unable to contact my friend. Shortly after receiving the death notice, I was passing the landscape scene for the fifth time. Until then I had not wanted to face the meaning of death in such a strikingly beautiful setting. I was unable to offer my support and sympathy, thus I put death out of action. Tacit surgings made death an instant reality and required that the cemetery be given its rightful place.

In illumination, it is just such missed, misunderstood, or distorted realities that make their appearance and add something essential to the truth of an experience. The illumination process has been continually recognized in creative discoveries from the earliest thinkers on science and is a key theme in Capra's *The Turning Point* (1982) and in Kuhn's *The Structure of Scientific Revolutions* (1970).

Explication

Once illumination relevant to themes, qualities, and components of a topic or question occurs, the heuristic researcher enters into a process of explication similar to (but in much more detail than) the effort described above to understand and explain the meanings behind the missed cemetery in the landscape scene.

The purpose of the explication phase is to fully examine what has awakened in consciousness, in order to understand its various layers of meaning. Numerous heuristic approaches are utilized in pursuing a full elucidation of the descriptive qualities and themes that characterize the experience being investigated. A comprehensive elucidation may also include the recognition of new constituents and themes. In the explication process, the heuristic researcher utilizes focusing, indwelling, self-searching, and self-disclosure, and recognizes that meanings are unique and distinctive to an experience and depend upon internal frames of reference. The entire process of explication *ie* requires that researchers attend to their own awarenesses, feelings, *self bias* thoughts, beliefs, and judgments as a prelude to the understanding that is derived from conversations and dialogues with others.

Perhaps the most significant concepts in explicating a phenomenon are focusing and indwelling, where concentrated attention is given to creating an inward space and discovering nuances, textures, and constituents of the phenomenon which may then be more fully elucidated through indwelling.

In explication a more complete apprehension of the key ingredients is discovered. Additional angles, textures, and features are articulated; refinements and corrections are made. Ultimately a comprehensive depiction of the core or dominant themes are developed. The researcher brings together discoveries of meaning and organizes them into a comprehensive depiction of the essences of the experience. The researcher explicates the major components of the phenomenon, in detail, and is now ready to put them together into a whole experience.

Creative Synthesis

The final phase of heuristic research is the process of creative synthesis. The researcher in entering this process is thoroughly familiar with all the data in its major constituents, qualities, and themes and in the explication of the meanings and details of the experience as a whole. The creative synthesis can only be achieved through tacit and intuitive powers. Once the researcher has mastered knowledge of the material that illuminates and explicates the question, the researcher is challenged to put the components and core themes into a creative synthesis. This usually takes the form of a narrative depiction utilizing verbatim material and examples, but it may be expressed as a poem, story, drawing, painting, or by some other creative form.

Knowledge of the data and a period of solitude and meditation focusing on the topic and question are the essential preparatory steps for the inspiration that eventually enables a creative synthesis. The major concepts that underlie a creative synthesis are the tacit dimension, intuition, and self-searching. The researcher must move beyond any confined or constricted attention to the data itself and permit an inward life on the question to grow, in such a way that a comprehensive expression of the essences of the phenomenon investigated is realized.

To sum up: Behavior is governed and experience is determined by the unique perceptions, feelings, intuitions, beliefs, and judgments housed in the internal frame of reference of a person. Meanings are inherent in a particular world view, an individual life, and the connections between self, other, and world.

The Validation of Heuristic Research

Since heuristic inquiry utilizes qualitative methodology in arriving at themes and essences of experience, validity in heuristics is not a quantitative measurement that can be determined by correlations or statistics. The question of validity is one of meaning: Does the ultimate depiction of the experience derived from one's own rigorous, exhaustive self-searching and from the explications of others present comprehensively, vividly, and accurately the meanings and essences of the experience? This judgment is made by the primary researcher, who is the only person in the investigation who has undergone the heuristic inquiry from the beginning formulation of the question through phases of incubation, illumination, explication, and creative synthesis not only with himself or herself, but with each and every co-researcher. The primary investigator has collected and analyzed all of the material—reflecting, sifting, exploring, judging its relevance or meaning, and ultimately elucidating the themes and essences that comprehensively, distinctively, and accurately depict the experience.

Bridgman (1950) emphasizes the subjective bases of validation, the dependence of validity on the judgment and interpretation of the researcher:

> The process that I want to call scientific is a process that involves the continual apprehension of meaning, the constant appraisal of significance, accompanied by a running act of checking to be sure that I am doing what I want to do, and of judging correctness or incorrectness. This checking and judging and accepting that together constitute understanding are done by me and can be done for me by no one else. They are as private as my toothache, and without them science is dead. (p. 50)

The heuristic researcher returns again and again to the data to check the depictions of the experience to determine whether the qualities or constituents that have been derived from the data embrace the necessary and sufficient meanings. The heuristic researcher's "constant appraisal of significance" and "checking and judging" facilitate the process of achieving a valid depiction of the experience being investigated. They enable the researcher to achieve repeated verification that the explication of the phenomenon and the creative synthesis of essences and meanings actually portray the phenomenon investigated. In such a process, as emphasized by Polanyi (1969), "certain visions of the truth, having made their appearance, continue to gain strength both by further reflection and additional evidence. These are the claims which may be accepted as final by the investigator and for which he may assume responsibility by communicating them in print" (p. 30).

Although the process involves returning again and again to the raw data and checking again and again the constituent meanings of the experience for comprehensiveness and essence—a rigorous and disciplined series of steps—Polanyi (1969) has emphasized that there are no rules to guide verification that can be relied on in the last resort; the scientist must make the ultimate judgment. The synthesis of essences and meanings inherent in any human experience is a reflection and outcome of the researcher's pursuit of knowledge. What is presented as truth and what is removed as implausible or idiosyncratic ultimately can be accredited only on the grounds of personal knowledge and judgment (p. 120).

In heuristic investigations, verification is enhanced by returning to the research participants, sharing with them the meanings and

essences of the phenomenon as derived from reflection on and analysis of the verbatim transcribed interviews and other material, and
seeking their assessment for comprehensiveness and accuracy. For
example, in Humphrey's (1989) recently completed research on the
constituents of the search for life's meanings, he mailed each research
participant the composite comprehensive description of the experience with a request that it be examined to determine whether or not
it included the essential qualities and meanings of their experiences.
Thirteen of his 14 co-researchers responded; 10 indicated that the
comprehensive statement of essences had captured their experience
fully and accurately, and that nothing further need be added. Three
stated that important qualities had been omitted relevant to the "dark
side" of searching for life's meanings, and that these were necessary
and essential to an accurate portrayal of the experience. Humphrey
states:

> I had thought that my heuristic exploration . . . had been thorough. . . .
> Fortunately, the step of participant validation highlighted the reduced
> emphasis on this aspect and I returned to an heuristic process concerning
> the dark side of my own search and also re-examined the research
> interviews. The result was that I significantly expanded the importance
> of this element of the search for meaning. (p. 65)

Having revised his comprehensive description of the experience of
searching for life's meanings, Humphrey (1989) resubmitted it; all
co-researchers agreed that the revised statement contained the essence
of their experience.

Another example of the validation process of heuristic research
comes from my own studies of loneliness. The publication of *Loneliness* (Moustakas, 1961) was a way of taking responsibility for the
depictions of lonely experience and lonely life, for the derived meanings and essences of the experience, and for the analysis of loneliness
into themes of the alienating loneliness of anxiety, existential loneliness, and lonely solitude.

I received about two thousand responses from readers of *Loneliness*
and *Loneliness and Love* (Moustakas, 1972), a publication in which I
expanded the meaning of the phenomenon. I reprint two of these—
from *The Touch of Loneliness* (Moustakas, 1975)—which exemplify the
kind of verification offered by readers who recognized the creative

and destructive paths of loneliness, themes that were elucidated in my research:

A Little Boy Part of Me

I want to say something about your book, *Loneliness*. I was the son of an army officer, and I went to West Point and spent seven years in a very numb and lonely existence as an army officer. It was during a time of intense loneliness that I first discovered and read your book, *Loneliness*, four and a half years ago. I had just split with my wife after ten years of marriage and I was very deeply into experiencing that tragic loss for the first time. Loneliness had been an emotion which I had always managed to outrun. I had discovered that if I did something important or impressive that people would make a fuss over me and I would not have to experience my own loneliness. Additionally, at age five, I became "man of the house" when my father left for World War II, leaving me in charge of my mother and telling me to take care of her and to "be good" and he would hurry home. I tried so hard to "be good," yet he didn't come home for four years. I didn't burden my mother and kept my loneliness deep within myself. On a lake in New Hampshire, when loneliness literally caught up with me after having outrun it for so long, I cried deeply; I went beneath the veneer of my tough shell and found a whole new part of the essence of me—a creativity. I wrote poems and a book and painted. And more important, I discovered a little boy part of me that had grown up early—a tenderness which West Point didn't exactly nourish. I find that this tender part of me, rather than the tough part, was a part my friends and I both cherish. I then discovered that rather than my toughness being my strength, as I had miscontrued it in the military, it was really my tenderness that was my strength. (pp. 46-47)

In Loneliness I Have My Own Dream

I am writing you as, perhaps, many others have, upon reading your book on loneliness. It was difficult for me to muster up the courage to lift the cover and enter a world that I feared would tell me what I didn't want to know.

In vain I've tried to build bridges. Despondent, confused, with no other alternative than panic and suicide I would commit myself to the prison-like cacophony and discord of a mental institution.

Loneliness . . . the word has always brought with it an air of apartness, as one removed from throbbing, pulsing day-to-day paces.

How can I tell you? Today in spite of all my need to love and be loved, I still prefer moments of relief . . . alone. I'm soft and pliable clay, but I, too, have my own dreams.

It is odd how I feared reading your book—dreaded finding myself there in among the pages—oh, the name is different and perhaps the age but too much is a part of *me*. The "me" no one knows, so deep, so buried that it only comes out in a peaceful moment, alone. In the peaceful moment I am free, free of pressure or panic. Deep, vibrant, warm, calm, enveloping a beauty that is trampled in the madness of *here* and *now*. Aloft, without vanity or smugness are tears of joy. Only then have I felt the peace and depth of my real self. (p. 27)

I close this section with a narrative that I was inspired to write in my personal journal during my heuristic searches into loneliness. It points to the freedom that the lonely search itself inspired within me, a voice that urged me to speak from the depths of being, to say what was central and needed to be expressed.

I awoke this morning to a soft and gentle rain, remembering a night not long ago when we paced back and forth while you struggled to come to terms with your dying.

I am writing to tell you how much you have given me in your presence, in your love, in your unqualified acceptance of me. When I came, you always recognized me in a distinctive way. Above all else, I felt I mattered to you. You never let anything—time, or place or person—interfere with that. So I have counted on you like the ground I walk on and the air I breathe. You were always there for me in the way the earth and the sky are always there. It simply never occurred to me that the day would come when I no longer would have your eternal faith, that for awhile I would lose the earth, the water and the air, that I would have to watch my own footsteps and accept as real the end of a beautiful melody, and of all music.

What grieves me now in this time of painful loneliness is that I never before put my feelings, my sacred valuing of you, into words! In all the other times it was always you who spoke, of how much I offered you, and all the while you were fully there for me. So I want to say clearly and strongly for now and for all the days beyond that you have given me a special gift of life itself, and I know it with my eyes and ears and with all my senses. I will always cherish the unique presence that is you.

CLOSING COMMENTS

Heuristic research is an extremely demanding process, not only in terms of continual questioning and checking to ensure full explication of one's own experience and that of others, but also in the challenges of thinking and creating, and in the requirements of authentic self-dialogue, self-honesty, and unwavering diligence to an understanding of both obvious and subtle elements of meaning and essence inherent in human issues, problems, questions, and concerns.

Having presented the basic nature of heuristics in its origins and meanings and having delineated its conceptual foundations as well as its core processes and phases, the next chapter revisits the concepts and processes as components of research design and as the basis for methodology. In later chapters, applications and examples of heuristics will be presented to offer additional guidance in how heuristic inquiry works in practice, in the actual process of conducting human science investigations, and in applications of heuristic methodology to psychotherapy.

3

Research Design and Methodology

In heuristic methodology one seeks to obtain qualitative depictions that are at the heart and depths of a person's experience—depictions of situations, events, conversations, relationships, feelings, thoughts, values, and beliefs. A heuristic quest enables the investigator to collect "excerpts or entire passages from documents, correspondence, records and case histories" (Patton, 1986, p. 187). The researcher gathers detailed descriptions, direct quotations, and case documentations. Such qualitative methods enable the researcher to derive the raw material of knowledge and experience from the empirical world.

QUALITIES OF HEURISTIC INQUIRY

Douglass and Moustakas (1985) compared qualitative research with the traditional paradigm, noting that traditional empirical investigations presuppose cause–effect relationships while the qualitatively oriented heuristic scientist seeks to discover the nature and meaning of the phenomenon itself and to illuminate it from direct first-person accounts of individuals who have directly encountered the phenomenon in experience. In the Douglass and Moustakas study, heuristic inquiry was contrasted with phenomenological research as follows:

(1) Whereas phenomenology encourages a kind of detachment from the phenomenon being investigated, heuristics emphasizes connectedness and relationship. (2) Whereas phenomenology permits the researcher to conclude with definitive descriptions of the structures of experience, heuristics leads to depictions of essential meanings and portrayal of the intrigue and personal significance that imbue the search to know. (3) Whereas phenomenological research generally concludes with a presentation of the distilled structures of experience, heuristics may involve

38

reintegration of derived knowledge that itself is an act of creative discovery, a synthesis that includes intuition and tacit understanding. (4) Whereas phenomenology loses the persons in the process of descriptive analysis, in heuristics the research participants remain visible in the examination of the data and continue to be portrayed as whole persons. Phenomenology ends with the essence of experience; heuristics retains the essence of the person in experience. (p. 43)

The focus in a heuristic quest is on recreation of the lived experience; full and complete depictions of the experience from the frame of reference of the experiencing person. The challenge is fulfilled through examples, narrative descriptions, dialogues, stories, poems, artwork, journals and diaries, autobiographical logs, and other personal documents. The heuristic process is congruent with Schopenhauer's (1966) reference to lyric poetry: the depicted is "also at the same time the depicter" (p. 248) requiring vivid perception, description, and illustration of the experience.

A typical way of gathering material is through interviews that often take the form of dialogues with oneself and one's research participants. Ordinarily, such an "interview" is not ruled by the clock but by inner experiential time. In dialogue, one is encouraged to permit ideas, thoughts, feelings, and images to unfold and be expressed naturally. One completes the quest when one has an opportunity to tell one's story to a point of natural closing.

In his essay "Toward a Science of the Person," Rogers (1969) describes his heuristic process. He states that

> within myself—from my own internal frame of reference—I may "know" that I love or hate, sense, perceive, comprehend. I may believe or disbelieve, enjoy or dislike, be interested in or bored by. . . . It is only by reference to the flow of feelings in me that I can begin to conceptualize an answer. . . . I taste a foreign dish. Do I like it? It is only by referring to the flow of my experiencing that I can sense the implicit meanings. (p. 23)

The crucial processes in heuristics (once one understands the values, beliefs, and knowledge inherent in the heuristic paradigm) are:
1) concentrated gazing on something that attracts or compels one into a search for meaning: focus on a topic or formulation of the question; and
2) methods of preparing, collecting, organizing, analyzing, and synthesizing data.

FORMULATING THE QUESTION

All heuristic inquiry begins with the internal search to discover, with an encompassing puzzlement, a passionate desire to know, a devotion and commitment to pursue a question that is strongly connected to one's own identity and selfhood. The awakening of such a question comes through an inward clearing, and an intentional readiness and determination to discover a fundamental truth regarding the meaning and essence of one's own experience and that of others.

Polanyi (1969) has stated that "it is customary today to represent the process of scientific inquiry as the setting up of a hypothesis followed by its subsequent testing. I cannot accept these terms. All true scientific research starts with hitting on a deep and promising problem, and this is half the discovery" (p. 118). Polanyi points to the imperative nature of the problem as such: "To see a problem is to see something hidden that may yet be accessible. . . . It is an engrossing possession of incipient knowledge which passionately strives to validate itself. Such is the heuristic power of a problem" (pp. 131-132).

Discovering a significant problem or question that will hold the wondering gaze and passionate commitment of the researcher is the essential opening of the heuristic process. The question as such (and the researcher's relationship to it) will determine whether or not an authentic and compelling path has opened, one that will sustain the researcher's curiosity, involvement, and participation, with full energy and resourcefulness over a lengthy period of time.

Feild (1979) emphasizes this value and the difficulty of achieving it:

> What keeps you from asking a real question? . . . it had never occurred to me that the majority of so-called questions I had asked before were merely spontaneous pleadings. They were not really based on experience and study. Now, after years of training, I could, as it were, feel the question within me, but for the life of me I could not get it into the right words . . . finding the exact question can be a subtle and difficult process. One word placed in one part of a sentence may produce an answer that in another part of the sentence will produce something entirely different. We have to learn to be so accurate with our questions that the answer is as clear and simple as possible. (p. 18)

In order to design a heuristic research study that will reveal the meanings and essences of a particular human experience in an accurate, comprehensive, and vivid way, it is essential that the (1979) question be stated in simple, clear, and concrete terms. As Feild suggests, it is necessary that the key words and phrases be placed in the proper order. The basic elements of the search are found in the primary words stated in the ordering of the question. The question as such should reveal itself immediately and evidently, in a way that one knows what one is seeking. The question itself provides the crucial beginning and meaning, the nature of the searcher's quest. The way in which the investigator poses the question will determine what fundamental events, relationships, and activities will bear on the problem.

A passage from Kant's *Critique* (1929) further emphasizes the significance of the question, per se:

> To know what questions may reasonably be asked is already a great and necessary proof of sagacity and insight. For if a question is absurd in itself and calls for an answer where none is required, it not only brings shame on the propounder of the question but may betray an incautious listener into absurd answers, thus presenting, as the ancients said, the ludicrous spectacle of one man milking a he-goat and the other holding a sieve underneath. (p. 97)

Without the question itself having the qualities of simplicity, concreteness, specificity, and clarity—as Kierkegaard exclaims in *Concluding Unscientific Postscripts* (1941)—it will lose itself into vagueness and indeterminateness and "fantastically becomes a something that no existing human being ever was or can be" (p. 169).

The question grows out of an intense interest in a particular problem or theme. The researcher's excitement and curiosity inspire the search; associations multiply as personal experiences bring the core of the problem into focus. As the fullness of the theme emerges, strands and tangents of it may complicate an articulation of a manageable and specific question. Yet this process of allowing all aspects to come into awareness is essential to the eventual formulation of a clear question.

The heuristic research question has definite characteristics:

(1) It seeks to reveal more fully the essence or meaning of a phenomenon of human experience.

(2) It seeks to discover the qualitative aspects, rather than quantitative dimensions, of the phenomenon.

(3) It engages one's total self and evokes a personal and passionate involvement and active participation in the process.

(4) It does not seek to predict or to determine causal relationships.

(5) It is illuminated through careful descriptions, illustrations, metaphors, poetry, dialogue, and other creative renderings rather than by measurements, ratings or scores.

An effective question in heuristic inquiry upholds the characteristics and values of heuristic research delineated above. Suggested steps in formulating the question include:

(1) List all aspects of particular interests or topics which represent curiosities or intrigues. Do this freely, jotting down questions and thoughts even if they are not complete.

(2) Cluster the related interests or topics into subthemes.

(3) Set aside any subthemes that imply causal relationships, and any that contain inherent assumptions.

(4) Look at all the remaining subthemes and continue to consider them thoughtfully until one basic theme or question emerges as central, one that passionately awakens your interest, concern, and commitment.

(5) Formulate it in a way that specifies clearly and precisely what it is that you want to know.

Recent questions developed for heuristic studies have included: What is the experience of growing up in a fatherless home? What is the experience of being sensitive? How do people perceive and describe the experience of synchronicity? What meanings are inherent in the precognitive dream experience? What is the experience of writing poetry? What is the experience of really feeling connected with nature? How do people perceive and describe the experience of rhythm in significant relationships?

When a genuine question has been formulated, then, as Pearce (1971) explains, "If you hold and serve the question . . . and you really believe in your question, it will be answered; the break-point will arrive when you will suddenly be 'ready'. Then you must put your hand to the plow and not look back; walk out onto the water unmindful of the waves" (p. 108).

The heuristic researcher is not only intimately and autobiographically related to the question but learns to love the question. It becomes a kind of song into which the researcher breathes life not only because the question leads to an answer, but also because the question itself is infused in the researcher's being. It creates a thirst to discover, to clarify, and to understand crucial dimensions of knowledge and experience.

Solving a problem means finding one's way. Like swimming, skiing, or playing the piano, it requires practice. To be able to swim one must enter the water, and to become a problem solver one learns to solve problems (Polanyi, 1962).

In heuristic research, the openness of the researcher in elucidating ✓ the question, clarifying its terms, and pointing to its directions provides the essential beginnings of the discovery process. From there, as Kierkegaard (1965) has so aptly stated, the researcher must strive to be humble and not hold a single presupposition, so as to be in a position to learn the more.

EXPLORING AND ANSWERING THE QUESTION

Having formulated the question and defined and delineated its primary terms and meanings, the next step is a careful and disciplined organization of methods for preparing to conduct the study. This step is followed by construction of methods and procedures to guide a collection of data that will illuminate an answer to the question. After the data are collected, they must be organized and presented in a way that depicts and illustrates the themes, meanings, and essences of the experience that has been investigated.

Methods of heuristic research are open-ended. They point to a process of accomplishing something in a thoughtful and orderly way that guides the researcher. There is no exclusive list that would be appropriate for every heuristic investigation, but rather each research process unfolds in its own way. Initially, methods are envisioned and constructed that will guide the research through the preparation phase and facilitate the collection and analysis of data. They facilitate the flow of the investigation and aim toward yielding rich, accurate, and complete depictions of the qualities or constituents of the experience. Keen (1975) has remarked that "The goal of every technique is to help the phenomenon *reveal itself more completely* than it does in ordinary experience. This goal may be stated as to uncover as many meanings as possible and their relations to one another as the phenomenon presents itself in experience" (p. 41).

As long as the method is congruent with responsible ethical concerns, any course that a researcher's ingenuity is capable of suggesting is an appropriate method for scientific investigation (Bridgman, 1950). Every method or procedure, however, must relate back to the question and facilitate collection of data that will disclose the nature, meaning, and essence of the phenomenon being investigated. This means methods and procedures that will yield accurate and vivid dimensions of the experience—situations, events, relationships, places, times, episodes, conversations, issues, feelings, thoughts, perceptions, sense qualities, understandings, and judgments.

Bridgman (1950) has emphasized that "science is what scientists do . . . there are as many scientific methods as there are individual scientists" (p. 83). The purpose of a method of scientific inquiry is to obtain an answer to the problem at hand. The working scientist, Bridgman observes, "is not consciously following any prescribed course of action, but feels complete freedom to utilize any method or device whatever which in the particular situation . . . seems likely to yield the correct answer" (p. 83). The heuristic researcher constructs methods that will explicate meanings and patterns of experience relevant to the question, procedures that will encourage open expression and dialogue.

Methods of Preparation

Common methods of preparation include immersion in the topic or question, going wide open to discover meanings in everyday observations, conversations, and published works. This requires that the researcher be alert to signs or expressions of the phenomenon, willing to enter a moment of the experience timelessly and live the moment fully. It requires "a tacit and passionate contribution of the person knowing what is being known," as Polanyi (1962) emphasizes, and this "is no mere imperfection, but a necessary component of all knowledge" (p. 312).

When I began to study loneliness it became the center of my world. Every event, every feature of my existence appeared to me to be connected with loneliness. I found loneliness everywhere in my waking life—for instance, as a crucial component of hospitalized children separated from their families, or as an inherent quality of making decisions that impacted importantly on other's lives. It became a significant focus of the people with whom I met in therapy—whatever their presenting problems—and of my reflections on my own life. I recognized loneliness as a necessary condition of solitude and creativity. My dreams were filled with lonely awakenings and encounters. I walked the streets at night and noticed especially isolated stars, clouds, trees, and flowers. I was once confronted and threatened with arrest by municipal police, who told me that I was violating a local ordinance and that solitary middle-of-the-night sojourns were forbidden. On one occasion I was actually escorted home with rotating, flaring lights illuminating my every step. Throughout the early days of my investigations, loneliness was the mainstream of my life and colored everything else, influencing the meaning of everything else.

This kind of personal, private immersion provides the initial essen- ✓ tial preparation for discovering the nature and essence of a particular experience. Another example of such immersion is presented in Blau's (1980) study of anger:

> The more I continue to read and speak to people with whom I come in contact, the more my interest and curiosity piques. When I experience anger, I am aware that my innate, fundamental expression has been colored by years of suppression and is not diverted into other affects and forms of behavior . . . my essential connection with anger has been tampered with and is now entangled in layers of ingested messages. I want to recontact and connect with my natural experience of anger. To do so, I need to look directly at the experience itself; not just my thought processes, bodily aspects of this emotion, or the specific behaviors that are emerging. I must consider the full and complete experience to arrive at a deeper more genuine understanding. (p. 14)

Methods of preparation in heuristic research include:

(1) *Developing a set of instructions* that will inform potential co-researchers of the nature of the research design, its purpose and process, and what is expected of them.

(2) *Locating and acquiring the research participants,* developing a set of criteria for selection of participants—for example, age, sex, socioeconomic and education factors, ability to articulate the experience, cooperation, interest, willingness to make the commitment, enthusiasm, and degree of involvement.

(3) *Developing a contract.* which includes time commitments, place, confidentiality, informed consent, opportunities for feedback, permission to tape record, permission to use material in a thesis, dissertation, and/or other publications, and verification of findings.

(4) *Considering ways of creating an atmosphere* or climate that will encourage trust, openness, and self-disclosure.

(5) *Using relaxation/meditation activities* to facilitate a sense of comfort, relaxation, and at-homeness.

(6) *Constructing a way of apprising co-researchers* during the "collection of research data" phase of the importance of immersion and intervals of concentration and respite. George Kelly's (1969) guidance is helpful here:

√ Each person who participates should at some point be apprised of what the "experimenter" thinks he is doing, and what he considers evidence of what. It is of equal importance to ask what the "subject" thinks is being done, and what he considers evidence of what. Since this can change during the course of the experiment, it is appropriate to ask "subjects" what their perception of the experimental design was at each important juncture in the experience. (p. 56)

Appendices A and B at the end of this chapter provide examples of instructions and agreements for use with co-researchers.

Methods of Collecting Data

A typical way of gathering material in heuristic investigations is through extended interviews that often take the form of dialogues with oneself and one's research participants. Ordinarily, such "interviews" are not ruled by the clock but by inner experiential time. In genuine dialogue, one is encouraged to permit ideas, thoughts, feelings, and images to unfold and be expressed naturally. The inquiry is complete only when the individual has had an opportunity to tell his or her story to a point of natural closing. At such a time, the primary investigator is ready to locate and interview others. Although in theory it is possible to conduct heuristic research with only one participant, a study will achieve richer, deeper, more profound, and more varied meanings when it includes depictions of the experience of others—perhaps as many as 10 to 15 co-researchers, often met for extensive, long interviews.

Patton (1980, pp. 197-198) presents three basic interviewing approaches that are employed in collecting qualitative data appropriate for heuristic research:

(1) The *informal conversational interview* that relies on a spontaneous generation of questions and conversations in which the co-researcher participates in a natural, unfolding dialogue with the primary investigator.

(2) The *general interview guide* that outlines a set of issues or topics to be explored that might be shared with co-researchers as the interview unfolds, thus focusing on common information to be sought from all co-researchers.

(3) The *standardized open-ended interview* that consists of carefully worded questions that all research participants will be asked.

Of the three methods, the conversational interview or dialogue is most clearly consistent with the rhythm and flow of heuristic exploration and search for meaning. Dialogue is the preferred approach in that it aims toward encouraging expression, elucidation, and disclosure of the experience being investigated. Jourard (1968) has shown that self-disclosure elicits disclosure; there may be moments in the interview process when the primary investigator shares an experience that will inspire and evoke richer, fuller, more comprehensive depictions from the co-researcher.

Dialogue involves cooperative sharing in which co-researchers and primary researchers open pathways to each other for explicating the phenomenon being investigated. This means receiving the other as a partner, accepting and affirming the other person. The persons in the heuristic interview must be willing to say freely what they think and feel relevant to the research question, and what emerges in their awareness when the phenomenon becomes the focus of their attention and concentration. Although general questions may be formulated in advance, genuine dialogue cannot be planned. Jourard (1968) has borrowed from Buber's writings to emphasize that "dialogue is like mutual unveiling, where each seeks to be experienced and confirmed by the other. . . . Such dialogue is likely to occur when the two people believe each is trustworthy and of good will" (p. 21). Buber (1965) expands on the values of dialogue:

> Where the dialogue is fulfilled in its being, between partners who have turned to one another in truth, who express themselves without reserve and are free of the desire for semblance, there is brought into being a memorable common fruitfulness which is to be found nowhere else. At such times, at each such time, the word arises in a substantial way between men who have been seized in their depths and opened out by the dynamic of an elemental togetherness. The interhuman opens out what would otherwise remain unopened. (p. 86)

√   In heuristic interviewing, the data generated is dependent upon accurate, empathic listening; being open to oneself and to the co-researcher; being flexible and free to vary procedures to respond to what is required in the flow of dialogue; and being skillful in creating a climate that encourages the co-researcher to respond comfortably, accurately, comprehensively, and honestly in elucidating the phenomenon.

Questions that a primary researcher might ask about a co-researcher include:

- What does this person know about the experience being studied?
- What qualities or dimensions of the experience stand out for the person? What examples are vivid and alive?
- What events, situations, and people are connected with the experience?
- What feelings and thoughts are generated by the experience?
- What bodily states or shifts in bodily presence occur in the experience?
- What time and space factors affect the person's awareness and meaning of the experience?
- Has the person shared all of the significant ingredients or constituents of the experience?

In the process of exploring these questions with research participants, the heuristic researcher is affected as Weber (1986) emphasizes:

> We cannot and should not be unaffected by what is said, unless of course we are either not listening or are simply denying what we feel under the false and smug cloak of scientific objectivity. . . . On the contrary it is only in relating to the other as one human being to another that interviewing is really possible . . . when the interviewer and the participant are both caught up in the phenomenon being discussed. (p. 68)

The researcher must keep in mind throughout the process that the material collected must depict the experience in accurate, comprehensive, rich, and vivid terms. In heuristic research, depictions are often presented in stories, examples, conversations, metaphors, and analogies. The interview should be tape-recorded and later transcribed. The basic data for illuminating the question and providing a basis for analysis of constituents, themes, and essences of the experience come from transcriptions and notes taken immediately following the interview.

To supplement the interview data, the heuristic researcher may also collect personal documents. Diaries, journals, logs, poetry, and artwork offer additional meaning and depth and supplement depictions of the experience obtained from observations and interviews.

Methods of Organizing and Synthesizing Data

Transcriptions, notes, and personal documents are gathered together and organized by the investigator into a sequence that tells the story of each research participant. Essential to the process of heuristic analysis is comprehensive knowledge of all materials for each participant and for the group of participants collectively. The task involves timeless immersion inside the data, with intervals of rest and return to the data until intimate knowledge is obtained.

Organizing and analyzing heuristic data during the immersion and incubation process may take many forms. Clark (1988), in his study of the psychologically androgynous male, describes a five-month process during which the core themes and patterns of his research gradually began to emerge and take shape. He listened to the interview tapes for several weeks before beginning to take notes on them; his detailed notes included extensive quotations and descriptions of material gathered during the interview, as well as their effects on the co-researchers.

After immersing himself in the tape and notes of each co-researcher, Clark developed a portrait of each participant's experience and later contacted them for feedback on the portraits. He received a positive response from each co-researcher affirming the accuracy of his depiction of their experiences. Three offered additional examples and qualities that they viewed as important; these were included in the final construction of their portraits.

As Clark continued to immerse himself in the data, he found it helpful to develop a diagram on which he placed the core qualities of being a psychologically androgynous male. The diagram was a kind of androgyny map which gave him a viewable panorama of over 200 components of the experience of the psychologically androgynous male. Clark utilized a color-coding system to cluster related ideas into a system of quadrants. He recounts the process in the following: "Some individual aspects of the experience appeared in more than one quadrant, but each quadrant represented a unique thematic matrix of closely connected components of psychological androgyny. The process of watching these quadrants take shape was fascinating" (p. 94).

When the androgyny map was complete, Clark spent several weeks alternately immersing himself in the phenomenon and engaging in other activities of work, play, and rest, noting that "during this time many shifts occurred in my perception of the map, and I began to note themes and relationships between ideas which had not been apparent previously" (p. 95).

Once knowledge of the question has been expanded and the investigator has lived with this knowledge for awhile, at some point an illumination will occur that facilitates the understanding and explication of essential qualities and themes. The insight or illumination is followed by a comprehensive explication of the core themes developed into an _individual depiction_ of each research participant's experience. The individual depiction may include descriptive narrative, examples, and verbatim exemplary material drawn from the tape-recorded interview. It also may include verbatim conversations, poetry, and artwork. From the totality of individual depictions a _composite depiction_ of the experience is constructed; then the heuristic researcher returns to the transcription of the tape-recorded interviews and the individual depictions constructed earlier. Through immersion and analysis of the individual data, two or three _exemplary portraits_ are developed, profiles that are unique to the individuals yet characterize the group as a whole.

Finally, the heuristic researcher develops a _creative synthesis_, an original integration of the material that reflects the researcher's intuition, imagination, and personal knowledge of meanings and essences of the experience. The creative synthesis may take the form of a lyric poem, a song, a narrative description, a story, or a metaphoric tale. In this way the experience as a whole is presented, and, unlike most research studies, the individual persons remain intact.

OUTLINE GUIDE OF PROCEDURES
FOR ANALYSIS OF DATA

(1) In the first step in organization, handling, and synthesizing, the researcher gathers all of the data from one participant (recording, transcript, notes, journal, personal documents, poems, artwork, etc.).

(2) The researcher enters into the material in timeless immersion until it is understood. Knowledge of the individual participant's experience as a whole and in its detail is comprehensively apprehended by the researcher.

(3) The data is set aside for awhile, encouraging an interval of rest and return to the data, procedures which facilitate the awakening of fresh energy and perspective. Then, after reviewing again all of the material derived from the individual, the researcher takes notes, identifying the qualities and themes manifested in the data. Further study and review of the data and notes enables the heuristic researcher to construct an individual depiction of the experience. The individual depiction retains the language and includes examples drawn from the individual co-researcher's experience of the phenomenon. It includes qualities and themes that encompass the research participant's experience.

(4) The next step requires a return to the original data of the individual co-researcher. Does the individual depiction of the experience fit the data from which it was developed? Does it contain the qualities and themes essential to the experience? If it does, the researcher is ready to move on to the next co-researcher. If not, the individual depiction must be revised to include what has been omitted or deleted, and what are or are not essential dimensions of the experience. The individual depiction may also be shared with the research participant for affirmation of its comprehensiveness and accuracy and for suggested deletions and additions.

(5) When the above steps have been completed for one research participant, the investigator undertakes the same course of organization and analysis of the data for each of the other research participants until an individual depiction of each co-researcher's experience of the phenomenon has been constructed.

(6) The individual depictions as a group, representing each co-researcher's experience, are gathered together. The researcher again enters into an

immersion process with intervals of rest until the universal qualities and themes of the experience are thoroughly internalized and understood. At a timely point in knowledge and readiness, the researcher develops a composite depiction that represents the common qualities and themes that embrace the experience of the co-researchers. The composite depiction (a group depiction reflecting the experience of individual participants) includes exemplary narratives, descriptive accounts, conversations, illustrations, and verbatim excerpts that accentuate the flow, spirit, and life inherent in the experience. It should be vivid, accurate, alive, and clear, and encompass the core qualities and themes inherent in the experience. The composite depiction includes all of the core meanings of the phenomenon as experienced by the individual participants and by the group as a whole.

(7) The heuristic researcher returns again to the raw material derived from each co-researcher's experience, and the individual depictions derived from the raw material. From these data, the researcher selects two or three participants who clearly exemplify the group as a whole. The researcher then develops individual portraits of these persons, utilizing the raw data, individual depictions and autobiographical material that was gathered during preliminary contacts and meetings, contained in personal documents, or shared during the interview. The individual portraits should be presented in such a way that both the phenomenon investigated and the individual persons emerge in a vital and unified manner.

(8) The final step in heuristic presentation and handling of data is the development of a creative synthesis of the experience. The creative synthesis encourages a wide range of freedom in characterizing the phenomenon. It invites a recognition of tacit-intuitive awarenesses of the researcher, knowledge that has been incubating over months through processes of immersion, illumination, and explication of the phenomenon investigated. The researcher as scientist-artist develops an aesthetic rendition of the themes and essential meanings of the phenomenon. The researcher taps into imaginative and contemplative sources of knowledge and insight in synthesizing the experience, in presenting the discovery of essences—peaks and valleys, highlights and horizons. In the creative synthesis, there is a free reign of thought and feeling that supports the researcher's knowledge, passion, and presence; this infuses the work with a personal, professional, and literary value that can be expressed through a narrative, story, poem, work of art, metaphor, analogy, or tale.

This presentation of heuristic research design and methodology has embraced beliefs, values, theory, concepts, processes, and methods that are essential to an understanding and conduct of heuristic research and discovery. Additional parameters of heuristics may be found in the chapter on "Heuristic Research" in *Individuality and Encounter* (Moustakas, 1968), in "Heuristic Methods of Obtaining Knowledge" in *Rhythms, Rituals, and Relationships* (Moustakas, 1981), and in the article "Heuristic Inquiry" (Douglass & Moustakas, 1985).

CREATING THE RESEARCH MANUSCRIPT

Once heuristic interviews have been completed, transcribed, organized, depicted, and synthesized, the research is nearing completion. At this point, it is time to present the research process and findings in a form that can be understood and utilized. The following outline for the manuscript, a guide for presentation of the work of an heuristic investigation, is offered as one way of bringing together an experience that has profoundly affected the investigator and which holds possibilities for scientific knowledge and social impact and meaning.

Introduction and Statement of Topic and Question

Out of what ground of concerns, knowledge, and experience did the topic emerge? What stands out as one or two critical incidents in your life that created the puzzlement, curiosity, passion to know? Does the topic have social relevance? How would new knowledge contribute to your profession? To you as a person and as a learner? State your question and elucidate each of the key terms.

Review of the Literature

Discuss the computer search, databases, descriptors, key words, and years covered. Organize the review to include an *introduction* that presents the topic reviewed and its significance; an *overview* and discussion of the methodological problems; *methods* that describe what induced you to include the published study in your review and how these studies were conducted; *themes* that cluster into patterns and which organize the presentation of findings; and *conclusions* that summarize core findings relevant to your research that differentiate your investigation from those in the literature review with regard to the questions, models, methodology, and knowledge sought.

Methodology

List and discuss methods and procedures developed in preparing to conduct the study, in collecting the data, and in organizing, analyzing, and synthesizing the data.

Presentation of Data

Include verbatim examples illustrating the collection of data and its analysis and synthesis. Discuss thematic structures and illustrate them, in addition to the themes themselves. Include depictions of the experience as a whole, and exemplary portraits that are vivid, comprehensive, and accurate. In the presentation of data include individual depictions, a comprehensive depiction, two or three exemplary individual portraits, and a creative synthesis.

Summary, Implications, and Outcomes

Summarize your study in brief, vivid terms from its inception to its final synthesis of data. Now that your investigation has been completed, how in fact do your findings differ from findings presented in your literature review? What future studies might you or others conduct as an outcome of your research? (Suggest a design in some detail for one or two future studies.) What implications of your findings are relevant to society? To your profession? To you as a learner and as a person? Write a brief, creative close that speaks to the essence of your study and its significance to you and others.

CLOSING COMMENTS

Heuristic research is a demanding and lengthy process. Once one enters into the quest for knowledge and understanding, once one begins the passionate search for the illumination of a puzzlement, the intensity, wonder, intrigue, and engagement carry one along through ever growing levels of meaning and excitement. A unique, temporal rhythm has awakened in one's absorption and sustaining gaze, a rhythm that must take its own course and that will not be satisfied until a natural closing occurs and a sense of wonder has fulfilled its intent and purpose. In Rourke's study of inspiration (1984), she points to the ways in which the knowledge obtained has enriched her life and that of others. Her kinship with the sea moved her to create a synthesis that energizes the possibilities of inspiration:

O sea that is known
Yet unfolding as mystery,
I live in you yet,
You fill my being.
A power I choose
not to resist,
A light dispelling
all darkness
exposing possibilities
of what can be.
You connect the fragments
of my experiences
enabling the flow
of my dynamic spirit,
transforming my limitations
into a highway of hope.
Transcending all that
is mundane,
I can not see that
better part of life.
You thrill me, enliven me,
reveal to me
all that I can be
charging me with courage
to be what I am
I am who I am.
I am inspired. (pp. 182-183)

Heuristic research processes include moments of meaning, understanding, and discovery that the researcher will hold and savor. Feelings, thoughts, ideas, and images that have been awakened will return again and again. A connection has been made that will remain forever unbroken and that will serve as a reminder of a lifelong process of knowing and being. Polanyi (1962) touches on this relationship: "Having made a discovery, I shall never see the world again as before. My eyes have become different; I have made myself into a person seeing and thinking differently. I have crossed a gap, the heuristic gap, which lies between problem and discovery" (p. 143).

APPENDIX A: INSTRUCTIONS TO
RESEARCH PARTICIPANTS

Date_____

Dear_____,

Thank you for your interest in my dissertation research on the experience of _____. I value the unique contribution that you can make to my study and am excited about the possibility of your participation in it. The purpose of this letter is to reiterate some of the things that we have already discussed and to secure your signature on the participation-release form which you will find attached.

The research model I am using is a qualitative one through which I am seeking comprehensive depictions or descriptions of your experience. In this way I hope to illuminate or answer my question: _____? The terms of my question, as I am using them, mean _____, _____, and _____.

Through your participation as a co-researcher, I hope to understand the essence of the phenomenon as it reveals itself in your experience. You will be asked to recall specific episodes or events in your life in which you experienced the phenomenon we are investigating. I am seeking vivid, accurate, and comprehensive portrayals of what these experiences were like for you; your thoughts, feelings, and behaviors, as well as situations, events, places, and people connected with your experience. You may also wish to share personal logs or journals with me or other ways in which you have recorded your experience—for example, in letters, poems, or artwork.

I value your participation and thank you for the commitment of time, energy, and effort. If you have any further questions before signing the release form or if there is a problem with the date and time of our meeting, I can be reached at _____. (Telephone Number)

Sincerely,

APPENDIX B: PARTICIPATION-RELEASE AGREEMENT

I agree to participate in a research study of _____, as described in the attached narrative. I understand the purpose and nature of this study and am participating voluntarily. I grant permission for the data to be used in the process of completing a Ph.D. degree, including a dissertation and any other future publication. I understand that my name and other demographic information which might identify me will not be used.

I agree to meet at the following location _____ on the following date _____ for an initial interview of 1½ to 2 hours, and to be available at a mutually agreed time and place for an additional 1 to 1½-hour interview, if necessary. I also grant permission for the tape recording of the interview(s).

_____   _____

Research Participant   Primary Researcher

_____   _____

Date   Date

4

Examples of Heuristic Research

Verbatim material from an initial interview and examples of individual depictions of experience, composite depictions, portraits, and creative syntheses are provided in this chapter. The primary purpose is to convey how heuristic research data is organized and presented; the nature, meaning, and essence of an experience from the vantage point of the person and group offering first-person accounts of their experience with the phenomenon.

EXCERPT FROM AN INITIAL INTERVIEW

Really Feeling Connected with Nature

In her study on connectedness to nature, Joan Snyder (1989) includes a verbatim account of the initial interview with a co-researcher. The opening excerpt from the complete text follows:

JOAN   What I am interested in is what your experience is in really feeling connected with nature. That may just be an outpouring of what things have happened in your life where you felt that connection. Or there may be some one particular experience that stands out over all of the rest of them. . . .

JOY   Yeah, I have a number of times when I have felt really connected to nature. The first one that I think of happened in 1979. I went out West alone to Estes Park and hiked the trails. I want to say more about the mountains later, but I wanted to focus on a particular morning that I hiked a trail into Quinland Lake. The path was steep up for a while and then gradually wound down again to a forest that you had to walk through on you way to the lake. I was walking along the trail, just moseying along the trail, and all of a sudden I

came to a tree that had been newly damaged. Either the wind had
taken out the top of it, or maybe it had been struck by lightning, I
don't know what happened to it. But the tree stood . . . it exposed
its core and its core was so beautiful in the sunlight. It was a tawny
golden light. The light seemed to come right out of it. The sun was
on it. There was a specialness . . . (hand to heart) . . . like a cathedral.
I walked up to it. I had to touch it and I cried . . . I had the sense
that things were going to be okay. I just stood there for quite a
while. . . . When I touched the tree I felt a warmth in my solar
plexus. The tree was saying "I know you". It was like a reunion. . . .
It was a Gestalt, a completion. . . . In my family system the way we
dealt with spirituality was to brush it aside and say, "feeling a little
hokey today." But I couldn't, I didn't want to brush it aside. The
feeling I got from that tree and the connection I got was to nature.
. . . It was something more than me . . . a promise. A nurturance, a
being there, a centeredness, a fulfillment. And it *was* in my heart,
right to my heart. I just had a feeling of peacefulness and calmness
throughout . . . God, the beauty of it, you know, like a beautiful
piece of wood that you can't, you just cannot keep your hands off.
I have to touch it, I have to feel it. I'm a tree hugger. I like to put my
face right up to the bark and put my arms around it. (pp 172-176)

INDIVIDUAL DEPICTIONS

The Experience of Touch in Blindness

This example of an individual depiction is from among many that
appeared in Lusseyran's *And There Was Light* (1987). Lusseyran's
account of his experience of blindness was first and foremost a search
to find meaning in blindness, to understand the phenomenon, and to
learn from it. In the excerpt, Lusseyran focuses on touch, the nature
and meaning of touch as affected by blindness (his own, and perhaps
that of all persons visually impaired).

Lusseyran (1987), who was blinded at an early age, depicts the
experience of touch with particular emphasis on the relationship of
touch to movement and pressure, as dominant themes:

When I had eyes, my fingers used to be stiff, half dead at the ends of my
hands, good only for picking up things. But now each one of them started

out on its own. They explored things separately, changed levels, and, independently of each other, made themselves heavy or light.

Movement of fingers was terribly important, and had to be uninterrupted because objects do not stand at a given point, fixed there, confined to one form. They are alive, even the stones. What is more they vibrate and tremble. My fingers felt the pulsation distinctly, and if they failed to answer with a pulsation of their own, the fingers immediately became helpless and lost their sense of touch. But when they went toward things, in sympathetic vibration with them, they recognized them right away.

Yet there was something still more important than movement, and that was pressure. If I put my hand on the table without pressing it, I knew the table was there, but knew nothing about it. To find out, my fingers had to bear down, and the amazing thing is that the pressure was answered by the table at once. Being blind I thought I should have to go out to meet things, but I found that they came to me instead. I have never had to go more than halfway, and the universe became the accomplice of all my wishes.

If my fingers pressed the roundness of an apple, each one with a different weight, very soon I could not tell whether it was the apple or my fingers which were heavy. I didn't even know whether I was touching it or it was touching me. As I became part of the apple, the apple became part of me. And that was how I came to understand the existence of things. (pp. 26-27)

From the transcribed interview of each co-researcher, combined with other available data, such as journals, diaries, and personal documents, an individual depiction of the participant's experience is constructed. Excerpts from individual depictions follow.

Transforming Self-Doubt into Self-Confidence

Prefontaine's individual depiction offers a picture of the descriptive meanings that are characteristic of the transformation that occurs in identity in moving from self-doubt to self-confidence. The depiction presents the constituents of the experience, as well as the ambiguities and conflicting qualities that distinguish it from other human experiences. Verbatim excerpts from Prefontaine's investigations are presented to portray the qualities of self-doubt and self-confidence, as well as a sense of the shift that is taking place.

The Depiction of Self-Doubt

I am experiencing a general malaise which seems to suggest that something is wrong with me and with my life. I am in considerable physical discomfort, with a great deal of tension and some pain. At times, I feel locked up inside myself.

I tend to be suspicious of others and I get skeptical when they suggest that I can change, or that my future can be different. People don't really know me or understand me. I get cynical if others present convincing evidence to support their claims which I cannot discount or dismiss. To my disbelief and amazement, others have told me that I am arrogant and hard.

I avoid people and new situations. I am afraid of the unknown. In most situations, most of the time, I feel out of place. I am never sure of myself and never certain of what I really want. To decide anything is always difficult. At times, it is positively painful. I tend to postpone and to avoid making decisions as long as I can. I usually wait for the normal course of events to decide the outcome of my life situation.

I am torn by ambivalent feelings—wanting and then not wanting. Those feelings are strong and fluctuate very quickly. I belittle myself by thinking that others are better than I am and can do things better than I can. In conflict situations, I usually blame myself and presume that I was wrong. . . .

I resolve to change a lot of things in my life. I think of those changes in global terms such as wanting to slow down or wanting to lose weight. I see them happening in some distant future when everything will be just right. Most days I know what I want to do but can't seem to do it. When I attempt some things, it's as if my body doesn't obey or cooperate. There is a big gap between what I want to do and what I actually achieve. . . .

I question my attitude and my approach to life. At times I think I'm too serious, at other times not enough. I don't seem to know when to be serious and when not to be serious. I feel very limited. I am convinced that I have to grow a lot before I can possibly help anyone. I have a long history of negative attitudes and these attitudes influence what I do today. In that way, I am handicapped. . . .

Movement to Self-Confidence

I try a new behavior. I hesitate and am afraid. But I decide to speak out in front of others. I am a bit surprised that it was not as as painful as I thought it would be. After that I feel a bit relieved. I have more of a feeling of belonging. I feel some new energy in my body. I did better than I had imagined. Others said I did OK.

I discover that even when I fail, I can recover. This time, I didn't worry as much about how I'll make out. I can relax a bit more and enjoy myself more. I don't put myself down as often as I used to. I'm beginning to believe in my own strength.

I now realize that others are struggling with many of the same things as I am. I risk showing more of my faults and good points. When I tell others how I feel I don't have to pretend as much or even to tell white lies about how I feel. I am feeling things that I hardly remember ever feeling. Some feelings are brand new for me. When I tell others how I feel, I notice that they pay attention to me. That leaves me feeling more powerful. . . .

When I think of how far I have to go, I get discouraged. I want to quit because I can't have it all, all at once. Sometimes I despair that I'll ever make it. It all seems so impossible. I have so little to offer and no way of communicating it. I hope I make it.

I am discovering new things about myself. I react in unexpected ways. Hard things sometimes come easily and easy things give me trouble. Much of the time I don't understand myself. I am feeling differently about myself. I notice that I feel confident in a way I have never felt before. My depression leaves me when I get involved with others. . . .

I am doing a number of things that I did not do before. I play more with my children. I am able to hear my spouse. We share more of our thoughts together. A number of people have become rather special to me. We have become special to each other. Others listen to me, they offer support and I feel more confident. I can rely on myself because I always do my best. I can trust myself. I have been given enough strength to succeed.

I have noticed small changes within me. I am more relaxed. I can share more feelings and honest emotion without embarrassment or fear of reprisals. When I do that, I trust myself more, respect myself more and believe in myself more.

I feel that I am back in the swing of things. I have laid new foundations
for my future. . . . How can I begin to describe it? I feel like a flower in a
garden—blooming. (pp. 113-118)

The Mother-Daughter Relationship

The individual depictions of two co-researchers examining the
mother-daughter relationship are presented in poetic form.

Mother (Benjei, 1988)

She wasn't the mother I wanted to have.
She didn't hold me and hug me
and only rarely kissed my hurts away.
Instead of whispered lullabies she practiced scales
and sung the notes of well-known musicals
scolding my childish songs innocently out of tune
unskillfully accompanied upon the little celeste.
But she did get me a puppy dog.

She wasn't the mother I wanted to have.
Instead of peanut butter and jelly
deliciously on Wonder bread
she gave me cream cheese on raisin nut loaf
and our meals were always balanced
even if it meant eating okra.
She wouldn't play "London Bridge Is Falling Down"
but longed for another part Off Broadway.
She took us five days a week for ballet lessons
and I learned to dance.

She wasn't the mother I wanted to have.
She practiced scripts and was always reading weighty books
instead of bedtime stories.
No one could beat her at Scrabble
and she constantly reminded me to pronounce my final "t's"
but she always knew how to spell the word I needed
and finally I became a Doctor of Philosophy.

She wasn't the mother I wanted to have.
She didn't like to sew or cook except for super salads
though she did tolerate my furtive attempts
at culinary accomplishment
little cakes of flour and water mixed
with more mysterious ingredients
and banked on top of the oil burner.
Sometimes I hid the confections under my bed.

She wasn't the mother I wanted to have.
She always insisted we be on time for breakfast and dinner.
And she spanked me when she caught me trying on her clothes
tilting in her flowered dress and shoes
before her boudoir mirror.
She was very fond of red
but later on I discovered a different style.

She wasn't the mother I wanted to have.
She embarrassed me because she laughed too loud
and told off-color jokes
and converted all other conversation into puns.
And she couldn't read my poetry the way that it was meant.
Now I know it was because
she couldn't touch the tears behind her smile.
I hardly ever saw her cry.

She wasn't the mother I wanted to have.
I went to school two thousand miles away
to be without her scathing scolding frequent anger.
So she mailed me a subscription to Time magazine
because she suspected I didn't read the news
and sent me care packages of fruit and cookies
and even a birthday cake, right on time.

She wasn't the mother I wanted to have.
And now as I sit in the house that she designed
a no longer new contemporary, once ahead of its time
even if it was painted turquoise and flamingo
I remember all the gatherings here.

I remember all the people
that have passed through this door
some, as her, that are no more

many that were strange, all that were welcome.
And thinking on my own ministry, and knowing how in part
that came to be
I am thankful that I did not have the opportunity
to choose a different
Mother.

An Ode to My Mom (Spivack, 1985)

I sit here basking in your sun.
Enveloped by its warmth, your warmth, feeling the warm energy
permeating every fiber of my soul.
And yet allowing a cool breeze to enter my being and rustle on my cheek
and through my hair.
And I, in return, can feel my warmth and energy meet yours.
And then a change occurs, a boat comes by, a bee buzzes in my hair.
The spell of the encompassing warmth is disturbed but I *know* that it is
there in part, and that's enough.
A cloud comes by, and it grows dark.
I can no longer see the sun or feel the heat, *but* it is there.
Not only behind the cloud waiting patiently for *me* to appear again.
But deep inside of me
You are part of me.
I am a part of you.
You will always nurture and love me and I, you.
We will never leave each other.
Our warmth will last forever.
Our sun will always shine.
A love so deep and wondrous cannot die.
And so it did not die.
I look into my daughter's eyes.
I feel her warmth and know that she feels mine. And so
Our love, dear mother, yours and mine
Lives on and on.
And so some day
Our Susan will look into her daughter's eyes and see our love, and see
her love with me and bring that love to her unborn child
Her love returned in full by eyes so trusting and so filled with joy.

And so my love, dear Mom, you are my child, my sun, my guiding light,
my source of love, my cloak of warmth
Our love so deep and wondrous will never die.

The Experience of Mystery in Everyday Life

The final individual depiction is derived from Varani's investigation of mystery. In this study, Varani (1985) explored the mystery of death, relationships, growth, and healing. The excerpts selected focus on the mystery that permeates interpersonal relationships. Varani recognizes that ordinarily mystery is not associated with friendships; on the contrary, he points out that usually people are consciously aware of the nature of their relationships. In his meditations and self-dialogues on mystery, however, Varani discovered that strong elements of the unknown entered into his own relationships. He felt in an intense way his vulnerability when he was challenged or criticized. He felt himself opened up, transparent, his inner world exposed. Ways in which mystery permeated his relations with others are as follows:

> As I was led away from my usual and familiar "self," I was being led to find my true self. This other person's frame of reference acts like a parable or a story that enlarges my own standpoint, and, as a result, I am plunged into areas I have disregarded, have chosen to ignore, or have failed to perceive existed. . . .

> It is this process which I have identified that enables me to uncover aspects of my life which I normally would not bother looking into. . . . In this struggle I have experienced the pain of my limitations and the sadness in failing to provide time and space. This pain symbolizes my commitment. Herein lies the mystery of my experience. Because I do not provide sufficient time to nurture my relationships, I can only rely on my faith in myself. I can only trust in my word which agrees to each relationship. I experience the mystery in the mutual freedom and mutual trust that is shared in the relationship by each individual.

> In reflecting upon the future of my relationships, I am also aware of mystery being present. My record of past relationships includes superficial ones, exploitive ones, and those which were terminated abruptly or which were still-born. I am aware of pain and hurt from these memories. There is a fear associated with the future of my relationships. I fear the unknown development or evolution of them; I fear whether I will be able to meet each one's demands. I sense here uncertainty. On the other hand, I also sense a confidence in myself that relationships will flourish, deepen, evolve, expand. I envision expressions of meaning will come as various levels of mystery are journeyed. In my journal I noted,

It (the future of the relationship) will be like the flowing of rivers at a deep source. . . . The relationship will emit rays of meaning as well as deeper mysteries. The life of the relationship will be sustained by the deeper meanings. . . . Meaning and mystery will accompany one another, it seems to me.

A final reflection on my experience of mystery in relationships is that the mystery deepens. As I enter into one mystery, I find myself plunging more deeply into other mysteries. It is my belief that as I enter into the mystery of another person in a relationship, "(I am) opened to the sense of ultimacy, that is, an experience of God. It seems to me that Life Itself is revealed to me". My experience of relationships in this deep sense has provided me a solid ground upon which the relationships stand. "A sense of being touched deeply in my being comes over me. Being so touched suggests . . . a deep movement at a level not focal to my awareness." (pp. 133-135)

COMPOSITE DEPICTIONS

The composite depiction of an experience is developed through a process of immersion into, study of, and concentration on the experience of the phenomenon as presented by each co-researcher. At some point in this process the qualities, core themes, and essences that permeate the experience of the entire group of co-researchers are understood and a universal depiction is constructed. The following examples illustrate the nature and character of the composite depiction.

The Experience of Being Sensitive

McNally's (1982) heuristic study ultimately focused on polar dimensions of sensitivity. In this excerpt from her research, she presents a composite depiction that includes contrasting themes of the experience of being sensitive. The two themes—the pain and anguish in sensitivity, and the awakening of wonder, awe, and feelings of love—depict a process that McNally believes is characteristic of sensitive people.

The experience of sensitivity involves feelings of being hurt and in pain. Although this seems to be the negative side of being sensitive . . . I see it as simply one side of the experience. It is an unpleasant, disturbing and difficult experience. It involves the core of the individual's self and is precipitated by being made fun of, by stresses in life, by separation from loved ones, by arguments with others we care about, by being criticized and rejected. The sensitive person feels attacked and is puzzled, uncertain and questioning. The body absorbs the pain, hurt, fear, anxiety, sadness, rage and anger. It is characterized by tightness, tenseness and a slumping, downward state. The person has taken in the assault and often becomes speechless and withdrawn. Weeping often accompanies the downward state of mind. The experience remains with the person and he/she feels crushed and devastated, "like being hit by a ton of bricks." There is a tendency to move away from the self. In addition, the images and feelings linger and stay with the person. (pp. 161-162)

Later in her composite depiction, McNally presents the positive qualities of being a sensitive person:

The person is touched inwardly, and there is a flow of life. The body is full and alive, glowing and at ease. Love, awe and wonder are the major feelings. There is an at-oneness, a peace and a light, upward energy. In a state of heightened awareness, the senses are sharpened and the person feels accepting, confident, strong, and important. It is a moment of inner awakening and of being alive. From this deepening and unfolding of the inner self, the person is moved toward a fundamental sense of communion with others. (p. 180)

Being Inspired

Rourke (1984) conducted an investigation of the nature and meaning of inspiration. In this excerpt she depicts the universal nature of the experience:

The experience of being inspired is an intrapersonal experience that is born out of a person's reflective encounter with self and one's life situation. It emerges from the individual's active sense of what is occurring in a life situation, a self engagement during a period of questioning, searching, struggling, or during a period of dispiritedness, grief, and pain.

Although the individual may undergo a long labor awaiting the arrival of the inspiration, ordinarily that actual moment of being inspired emerges suddenly. It usually takes the inspiree by surprise, creeping up like a "thief in the night." . . .

The experience of being inspired enters one's awareness with the recognition of a vital force or power. . . . One feels at home, where one has been out of control, able to act, a sense of being empowered. . . .

The power is impelling. It moves or drives the inspired person toward a certain goal. It presses for action. It incites new ideas. It urges one to embrace its cause. The power is also compelling. It demands the total attention of the inspired person. It commands absorption in the moment of its emergence. It leaves the inspired person with a "must," a "have to," a "pressure."

The felt-illumination integrates in such a manner that one feels directed. The sense is that of seeing what one must do, knowing how to do it, and having the will to carry it through. One feels like a runner on a definite course who has no doubt that the race will be finished because one is running on a mysterious or spiritual inner strength.

As this integration occurs, one begins to have the felt-sense of being transformed. . . . As the impulse of an inspiration arises in consciousness, one is empowered to move from wish to want to will to action without experiencing any blocks in the process. One experiences the dramatic inner movement of: "I see, I can, I will" that completely conquers the dispiritedness. . . .

For this moment of being inspired, brief or lasting, one feels uplifted as if one is seeing life from a mountain peak and the vision that one sees is powerful enough to sustain one's determination to finish the journey of the inspired action. It is as if for one brief moment one is able to rise above the mundane and the limitations of life and see its meaning in an extraordinary way. There is a magical mystical, ecstatic quality in this experience. (pp. 166-168)

The Experience of Self-Reclamation

Schultz (1983) interviewed twenty former Catholic religious women who had lived in religious communities over a period of six to fourteen years. She herself had been a nun. Utilizing heuristic processes and methodology and including herself as a research participant, Schultz studied the experience of reclaiming one's self in life outside the religious institution. Schultz offers a composite depiction based on the totality of individual depictions derived from her 21 co-researchers:

> The experience of self-reclamation as described by former Catholic religious women involved the following basic components: the experience of disillusionment and felt frustration of basic needs; the decision to fulfill basic needs by leaving the situation in which these needs were frustrated; the implementation of strategies in the development of personal capacities which were surrendered, disowned, or denied; and the incorporation of aspects of self into one's personal identity. . . .
>
> The experience of disillusionment involved a process of initial doubting of one's ideals, a search for the confirmation of one's ideals, and a letting go of one's ideals. During this process participants experienced a felt frustration of their basic needs for love and affection, and independence. An integral part of the process of disillusionment was the examination of one's ideals, one's actual experience of self and community, and the recognition that one's basic needs could not be fulfilled by remaining in the community.
>
> The decision to fulfill one's basic needs was expressed in the act of leaving the situation in which one was disillusioned and one's basic needs were frustrated. Leaving was experienced as an ending event in which participants gave up a familiar social identification, a pattern of life, and a social network. They were launched out into the unknown. Leaving was also an act of choosing to fulfill one's actual self rather than idealized images of self.
>
> Participants implemented strategies to develop personal capacities which had been surrendered, denied, or disowned. They developed their capacities of assertiveness, responsibility, freedom, and acceptance of self and others, through employing strategies which included looking for and securing employment, financial self-support, establishing a social network, and critically examining religious attitudes and practices.
>
> Development of one's personal capacities evolved through an increased awareness of one's needs, and engaging in activities which would enable one to fulfill these needs. (pp. 109-111)

The Meaning of the Precognitive Dream Experience

In a heuristically guided study of the meaning of the precognitive dream experience, Potts (1988) recorded and studied her own precognitive dreams as well as that of other dreamers. Her analysis included an examination of the impact of precognitive dreams on the personal, interpersonal, and social lives of the dreamer. The following excerpt reflects her compositive depiction of the meanings inherent in precognitive dreams.

> Within the transpersonal perspective, my co-researchers and I have experienced the restructuring of emotional attitudes toward ourselves and others through our precognitive dream experiences. Our precognitive dream metaphors have been imbued with the healing property naturally available to us to facilitate our emotional healing and movement toward wholeness . . . [and] meaningful feeling-connections with others have enabled us to transcend self. Expanded awareness through our precognitive dreams has led my co-researchers and me to personal and social transformation. Our precognitive dream experiences have ignited and released a multiplicity of felt feelings, potentiating expanded awareness and new possibilities for being. . . .
>
> The manner in which the dreamer constructively utilizes a precognitive experience depends upon the dreamer's attunement and appreciation of the dream and the meaning the experience has had for the dreamer. Effective utilization of precognitive dream experiences is related to the dreamer's sensitivity to and interest in dreams. By making individuals aware of their connections and disconnections to others, precognitive dreams contribute to a common human need for social vigilance. By sensitizing and elevating the dreamer's state of social alertness and self awareness, precognitive dreams facilitate the dreamer's positive restructuring of interpersonal and social relationships. This can lead to an increased capacity for love, understanding and compassion.
>
> Precognitive dream consciousness is a resource which calls to us. Our response to the call depends on several factors. Personal and social values are among the more important factors. The value an individual places upon dream consciousness can be a crucial determining factor. Societal values, which are reflected by social acceptance or rejection of precognitive dream experiences, are also determining factors. (pp. 249-252)

Growing Up in a Fatherless Home

Cheyne (1989), whose father was killed during World War II, studied her own experience of growing up in a fatherless home and that of other women who were raised without fathers. From her data, she developed a composite depiction of what it means to be without a father throughout one's childhood and adult life.

The female raised in a home devoid of a father's presence reflected a symphonic arrangement of themes which wove in and out of her life. Growing up in a fatherless home, she felt different from her peers who were raised in intact families. She envied and was in awe of these children because of the "wholeness" of their intact nuclear family structures. When she was invited to their homes, she often felt like a token child. It was like they were doing her a favor.

Throughout her formative years and into the present was the depressing feeling that there was something missing in her life. There was a sense of incompleteness, like a circle with a piece missing. This gap, this void, this need unfulfilled, penetrated the essence of her being and was omnipresent. . . .

Special days without her father's presence were particularly traumatic; not having her father there to walk her down the aisle on her wedding day, graduation, holidays, Father's Day, school functions and a host of other activities involving fathers and daughters were intensely painful reminders of her fatherless existence. A longing sadness permeated the core of her being; there were too many times that she missed her father— to hold her, to hug her, to protect her, to tell her she was pretty, that he loved her and that everything was, and would continue to be, OK. . . .

Father absence influenced and affected her relationships with males. She was often shy and uncomfortable with men, never knowing what to expect or instinctively how to act. Lack of positive reinforcement about her feminity compounded her difficulties relating to males with appropriate ease and confidence. She sought strength in males, finding herself attracted to those who presented a charismatic, "take charge" attitude; however, she was often disappointed as her heroes crumbled with their "feet of clay."

The fatherless female grew up with a lack of trust in males. She was hesitant about male/female relationships; afraid that she would be abandoned again. She sought nurturance from the male but approach-avoidance was the pattern, as she struggled with ambivalent and paradoxical feelings. This produced a situation that made establishing intimate relationships difficult. Making an emotional commitment to a male was fraught with danger. She was fearful of intimate undertakings because she had a need to remain in control.

In relating to men she found herself seeking the perfect male—one who had all the qualities she had unrealistically hoped for in her father. She was inevitably disappointed when men did not live up to her expectations and illustrious images. . . .

And, in the end, after all was said and done, the fatherless female with all her emotional pain, with all her feelings of alienation and insecurity, with all her resentment relating to her abandonment, was still ready to forgive her father—"the man who got away." (pp. 126-130)

The Experience of Shyness

From her heuristic investigations of shyness MacIntyre (1983) offers a composite depiction in the first person based on individual depictions of the entire group of her twenty co-researchers. Key elements of shyness include self-doubt, feelings of inferiority, bodily restraint and withdrawal, flushed face, accelerated heartbeat, heightened temperature, perspiration, anxious thoughts, internal critical absorption, embarrassment and non-assertiveness:

You want me to describe what happens. I feel that my whole bearing changes. As a matter of fact I am convinced that it does. I feel that I am getting flush in the face and my stomach is tied in a knot. Things just seem to be speeding; it is an adrenalin feeling. I think that everything is just rushing and pumping all through my system. I can almost hear my heart beat back and forth. I am not relaxed. I think that my voice quivers a bit; I know that it is barely audible. My eyes—I avert them. I find it hard to look someone in the eye. All the anxiety levels, the breathlessness—I try to take a deep breath. I really perspire. It as though someone suddenly turned on a lot of lights, like on a stage.

My mind is racing. One thought follows another in steady succession. I am constantly thinking about what to do. I am constantly talking to myself. I wonder whether I am doing things right and whether I will please people. Am I saying what these people want me to say? Am I performing as I should? Will I be successful? Often I will be quite negative with myself; I will put myself down. In my mind I will say: "I can't do this. I'm stupid. They're smarter than I am."

I feel afraid when I am shy. I almost hate to use the word, "afraid." Recently I had to speak before a group. I can remember feeling really afraid to do that and then getting up and doing it and feeling really relieved afterwards. Shyness is a feeling of anxiety too when I am not totally in charge of myself or of the situation. And I feel quite nervous— just worked up and nervous. My hands are soaking wet practically, I am so nervous. Sometimes I feel very angry and frustrated for I have been dealing with this for such a long time.

I prefer to be inconspicuous. When I join a new group I just sort of try to get in as unnoticed as possible. When others draw attention to me I am thinking desperately: "Oh God, stop. Why are you doing this to me? Just leave me out of this." When I feel shy I draw back from others. . . .

Deep down I know that I doubt myself. I have always had doubts about myself. If I am at home in my own surroundings, no problem, I feel very confident there. But feelings of self-doubt and instability recur. I have difficulty revealing myself to others and I believe there's a lack of self-esteem, a lack of self-confidence that goes along with that. Of course I would never feel like a total authority on anything. . . . I tend, therefore, to look upon others as superior to me. It's God on top, the neighbor next and me on the bottom. . . .

Shyness inhibits me. It is an experience that I try to cover up. I think of ways that I can hide it so nobody will notice and I am not enjoying this particular bit of excitement. Shyness is a feeling of holding back that affects my ability to concentrate, to focus and to think clearly. It also shrouds my personality. I think it is better than it used to be because I have gotten a little bit better appreciation for myself. Still I am always amazed that right out of the blue I can become so shy. It is so sudden. I would like to overcome shyness but I seriously doubt that I will completely overcome it. Perhaps I will have to learn to accept it; perhaps it is part of me. (pp. 153-157)

EXEMPLARY PORTRAITS

Based on the individual depiction but supplemented by demographic and autobiographic material collected during the preparation and collection of data, the primary investigator develops individual portraits of each co-researcher's experience. In the following section, exemplary portraits are presented to illustrate the retaining of the person's experience in the process of conducting and completing heuristic research.

Alicia—Return to Culture

Rodriguez (1985) investigated the nature, meanings, and qualities of ethnic identification of 15 Mexican Americans residing in San Diego County, one of whom was himself. The interviews focused on the co-researchers' perceptions, thoughts, feelings, beliefs and values that they considered as essential elements of the experience of cultural return. As part of his analysis, Rodriguez constructed portraits of each research participant's experience of the phenomenon, thus not losing the individual persons in the presentation of data. One of these portraits is selected here as exemplary of what cultural return is and means.

> Alicia grew up in a Mexican American bordertown in the South. She left the community to attend the state university, and she later taught high school on the East Coast of the United States. Alicia returned to the borderland areas of the South and the Southwest. Her return to the borderland areas is described in the following summary of her interview.
>
> > Culture for me is something that I live with on a day to day basis. Our Mexican American culture is something that perhaps all of us are constantly searching for. We are not necessarily away from it, but always trying to get a better grasp of it. There are experiences that I have had which provided the contrast for me to better define myself, my perceptions, and values which come from a Mexican American cultural base. These experiences in the long run have strengthened my understanding of my cultural background. I don't feel that I've ever experienced a real rupture with my culture. Growing up in a

dominant Mexican American community with a strong family influence cemented Mexican American culture as an important part of my life. At times I have entered into life experiences where striking differences with Anglo society were present or my contact with Mexican American people was limited. When I reentered the mainstream of Mexican American life, I was struck with the strong presence of my unique cultural background.

In situations where I was working or living within the dominant Anglo society, fortunately I could rely on Mexican American social networks which gave me a sense of closeness with Mexican American people, and identity in doing things. Having interaction through Spanish was an important link. For me, it's impossible to separate language from culture. I have also become more prone to do code switching. This involves the use of Spanish and English words together to transmit ideas to other bilingual people. I consider code switching one unique feature of contemporary Mexican American life.

I made conscious choices which have brought me into a firm grip with my self-identity as a Mexican American. All my choices seem to have brought me closer to working with Mexican American people. My college studies in Mexico and Spain broaden my sense of pride in my Mexican and Spanish heritage. I experienced a natural affinity for Mexican people, enjoyed interacting with them. While in Mexico I also developed an appreciation and pride in Indian culture. While I was on the East Coast and geographically removed from Mexican Americans, I made conscious efforts to seek out contact with other Hispanics. I later decided to teach in border cities such as Laredo and San Diego. As a teacher in the rural Mexican American community, I experienced the children as quiet and friendly, warm and respectful in a familiar way. Being a teacher was a special privilege, and I was accepted almost as a family member.

I decided to pursue a masters program involving Chicano studies. I later taught Chicano studies to high school youth. I was excited about working with youth who were aspiring to study their heritage and obtain greater awareness about themselves. As I reflect on my learnings of Mexican American life, two areas stand out. One important area involved the inclusion of mysticism and spirituality. The other area was the importance of the family. I feel the Mexican American family values closeness and intimacy.

The sum of my life choices and decisions have brought me into the profession of bilingual education. I find that the profession itself is a support system for full integration of Mexican American ways in daily work and living.

Alicia's experience crystalized perceptions of her unique cultural presence. Her return inspired greater recognition of the importance of cultural connections in her life as well as the lives of other Mexican Americans. Alicia's experience of return centered her in a particular professional field which sustained cultural frameworks. (pp. 186-188)

Edward—Psychologically Androgynous Male

Clark (1988) conducted extensive interviews with 11 male research participants who identified themselves as androgynous, one of whom was himself. His research was guided by four heuristic phases: immersion in the topic, including review and assessment of the published literature; explication of the philosophical, scientific, and psychological bases of heuristic inquiry; collection and analysis of data from which depictions and portraits were constructed; and synthesis of the essences of the experience of the psychologically androgynous male. From his extensive analysis, his portrait of Edward is chosen here to present the person within the experience.

Edward is a 35-year-old counseling agency administrator. He is soon to enter his second marriage and has no children. He described at length his process of growing self-awareness, during which he grew beyond the emotional structures he incorporated from his family-of-origin and developed a balance of his male and female attributes. He characterizes his journey toward self-awareness and self-directedness as a long and intense struggle, which has been helped immensely by his involvement in psychotherapy. Only during the past few years has he begun to experience the rewards of the struggle: feeling the freedom to experience and express his feelings, being capable of an emotionally intimate relationship with a woman, feeling personally powerful, feeling autonomous yet deeply involved in relationships, feeling the courage to open himself to change and growth.

Early in his adolescence he became aware of his androgyny, though he did not have a name for it. He felt different than most of his male peers, more sensitive, more empathic, placing high values on feminine traits.

He was never comfortable in all-male groups, especially when they displayed aggressive or misogynistic behavior. He found it easier to talk with females than males.

At many times during his life he has felt envy toward more traditionally-oriented males for their "pat" lives—their adherence to the structure of the male sex role and their apparently stable and painless lives as a result of doing what was expected of them by themselves and others. Though he thought, as he progressed on his growth process, that he was living a fuller, richer, and more interesting life than many of those men, he often wished his life contained less struggle and pain, and that he had models and societal guidelines so he did not have to create his way of being seemingly from scratch.

As he has become increasingly self-aware—that is, conscious of his feelings, thoughts, and behavior on an on-going basis—he has felt increasingly free to become the person he wants to be, rather than fulfilling expectations of his family-of-origin, peers, or the culture in general. He has also felt increasingly free to think or feel anything he wants without guilt or self-deprecation, free to feel fully responsible for his own life and not responsible for the feelings of others, free to fully utilize his thoughts and feelings to make decisions and choices, and free to balance his attachment to others and separation from others.

In his work on personal growth he has emphasized his relationship with himself, believing that he can essentially shape his life as he wants it, develop the courage to experience the full range of human feelings, and consciously decide the extent of his commitment to nurturing his own androgyny. He has realized that the less he tries to control people and situations the more control and ease he feels as a person. He has come to value and encourage his "natural flow"—that is, his intuitive abilities—which are enhanced by his awareness of his own feelings, moment to moment.

His androgynous experience in relationships with others has included choosing to associate or become intimate with other androgynous or unconventional people and being increasingly willing and able to risk emotional intimacy with another person.

He sees his experience as an androgynous male as voluntary immersion in a struggle to become a complete person. Essential to this immersion is his realization that change and growth is the natural rhythm of life, and that he can choose to be receptive to it and welcome it, rather than trying to stop or limit change or hang on to outmoded and ineffective ways of being. Androgyny, for him, is being committed to living life fully, including the willingness to fully experience both joy and pain, with a sense of readiness to change and grow. (pp. 140-142)

Lola—The Experience of Synchronicity

In Marshall's (1987) study, synchronicity was defined as the simultaneous occurrence of a psychic state—such as a dream, idea, or premonition—and one or more external events that are meaningful parallels to the psychic state. His eleven participants described the synchronous experience as involving great fear or terror. From the wide range of data that were developed into a composite depiction, portraits of the co-researchers, and a creative synthesis, an excerpt from Marshall's presentation of Lola is used here to illustrate this method of heuristic analysis.

Lola's synchronistic experience began with an initial warning that frightened her intensely. She had dreamt that her brother had been shot down over enemy territory. When she heard from her father that her brother was missing in action, she was literally petrified. Despite the lack of specific knowledge and in a state of shock, she was attuned to a gut reaction that her brother was going to escape serious injury.

Later on Lola discovered that her brother's plane had been shot down on the very night, on the very hour that she had the dream. She felt an immediate sense of amazement accompanied by skin-tingling sensations.

This experience lifted into awareness her tacit sense of knowing without concrete evidence or even awareness of how she knew, beyond any immediate or present realities. Her sense of being was not limited by her preconceptions. By freely entering into the synchronistic experience, she launched into a special relationship with her brother. By fearlessly turning away from her preconceptions, the split between outer and inner disappeared. She knew that he brother was alive, and that they would continue to share a life.

Through the years, following this synchronistic event, Lola has . . . felt connected with her family, especially her brother, despite the distance of time intervals between visits. Her synchronistic experience launched her utilization of the tacit sense in expanding her consciousness of the lived world and her sense of truth regarding events and relationships. (pp. 80-81)

Peter—Rejecting Love

Robert Snyder (1988) investigated the experience of rejecting love, with himself and nine other participants as the co-researchers. He gathered his data through tape-recorded interviews and dialogues utilizing qualitative methodology and the extended or long interview. In the process, he discovered that none of the co-researchers rejected the simple and pure gift of love, but rather the love that had expectations or strings attached, the love that was conditional. His portrait of Peter captures core qualities and themes of the experience of rejecting love.

Peter's portrait of the experience of rejecting love was initiated with his statement,

> I don't think I have ever genuinely experienced love with my family, my Mom and Dad. I experienced their physical caring for me, but love, it was a conditional sort of thing. If I had done something particularly winsome, they would recognize me, but most of the time the things I was doing weren't particularly winsome, and I felt the cold shoulder.

When I asked Peter to talk about the conditionality he replied,

> This whole thing is steeped in illusion and time. I am an actor in a family that has some legend to it. Socially it is very prominent and there are sort of expectations attached to the prominence. We don't do this like they do, we don't do that like someone else might. When we speak it has to be well received. We can't allow ourselves this or that because of what they might think. Just a lot of spotlighting. . . . The family messages as I interpreted them spelled out, 'Peter you have a self-worth and are lovable as long as your performance is excellent.' I never ever got a sense of comfort from Mom. I think more than anything else Mom was uncomfortable with my discomfort and Mom avoided it and denied it. 'I don't know what to do with your upset Peter, so don't have it. Let's pretend that it's not there.'

In view of all of such experiences, Peter found communion with nature:

I have always thought it was easier to love a sunset than a person. As a child, we would spend weekends up north at some cabins on a lake. I welcomed the seclusion and the solitude. I had all my friends—the pine trees, mocking birds, whip-poor-wills, beavers, fish, lake, sunsets, hill, stars, all my buddies, in their places, and I could count on that and it was easy to enter into our rhythm together.

I asked Peter to describe a specific experience of rejecting love. He told this story:

I can remember taking Peg to the local movie theater. I remember sitting next to Peg and feeling almost radioactive, like there was a real glow in me. It was sort of a magical moment. I think I just fell in love without committing myself. My body stood out for me, that was real clear in my mind. I cried in the movie. The crying at first I thought was just mirth and enjoyment, but then it was like I was recognizing some other meaning in my tears, and I was sure that some part of me was going to wreck my enjoyment. After the show, I continued to have this glow and this conflict and this apprehensive feeling. After the show we walked out of the theater and across the street to the fountain. . . .

I felt myself hardening and my lightness was leaving me and a heaviness seemed to be taking over. Before we got to the fountain, I quite clearly made up my mind that not only was I not going to ask her to marry me, but I was going to stop seeing her. I was going to end the relationship altogether. I think that really woke me up to my own terror of relating, and intimacy. So clearly, the chat I shared with Peg at the fountain was anti-climactic in the magical moment of things, and I saw a hurt expression sweep like a bitter frost across the contours of her face. I know she recognized, without my putting it into words, that I pulled back forever. There I was thinking, God damn it, here I am again I have hurt this person. You know there is some part of me that is all screwed up. Love just isn't in the books for me. I really had a sense of failure. Just abject worthlessness. All of the wonderfulness of the movie theater left me. I was very much alone at the fountain with Peg.

Since the painful encounter with Peg, Peter learned much about himself. The following more recent experience of rejecting love describes the shift. Peter shared,

Every now and then when I am feeling close with my wife, I will pull back suddenly and it will surprise me, and this moodiness will start to come out, and it's almost like a whip, and I will recognize the issue is mine, nothing my wife has done; it is my scaredness of closeness, and I will handle it with my wife. I am not stopping myself with these instances anymore. She will present herself in a way I am imagining is particularly vulnerable, where she is fully trusting, in my receiving her and being with her. Sometimes her openness scares me. I feel scared by the completeness of her trust. And then, I back off all of a sudden. It is almost like I had the experience of my wife being part of me, being inside me, and my boundaries were diffuse, and I wanted to define them. It was like, I can't be a puddle with another puddle, I will lose everything. I think that is my pulling back, to strengthen my sense of who I am. It is not the same as when I pulled back at the fountain. The terror is gone. I am still uncomfortable on occasion but the terror isn't present anymore. (pp. 90-95)

Bob—Interaction Rhythms

Robert Shaw (1989) has been fascinated with the nature of rhythmic interactions from his earliest memories. This compelling interest came into passionate focus when he found himself absorbed with the ease and flow of life between two persons when they were creating a bond or—its opposite—blockage of interactions when the rhythms were distorted or jarred by impaired communications. His investigation involved extensive interviewing of eight men and women and of himself as a way of systematically examining the phenomenon and discerning its qualities, primary themes, and essences. Excerpts from his own self-inquiry are an illustration of a portrait growing out of heuristic inquiry into a significant human experience.

In the past several years my interest in the phenomenon of rhythm has expanded to include a fascination with rhythmic ways in which people come together. . . .

When I was a youngster, I was taken up with athletics. When I look back and consider what has been and continues to be enjoyable for me about athletic participation, certain aspects are notable. I noticed that the sports which I enjoyed most were those in which I was participating with only

one other person. Although I enjoyed winning, the competitive component was less important or attractive to me than the establishment of a
particular series of interactional rhythms with that other person. Generally, I found it unpleasant to play tennis with someone who was always
trying to score a point, in any way possible. This is usually someone who
varies the pace too radically for me to fit in. I enjoyed playing with
someone who created with me a rhythmic exchange, who varied the
rhythm in ways that I was able to anticipate. A "winning" experience for
me would not be accumulating points against the other player, as much
as creating a symphony of movement or dance.

In looking back, I have discovered that in the most significant periods of
my life, I have had one or more regular partners with whom I have shared
a racquet sport. In my early teens, I spent endless hours at the home of
my best friend, playing ping-pong. Jerry played steadily and deliberately.
One point might last for ten minutes. How I loved anticipating his moves
and the rhythmic sounds that came when the ball made contact on each
side of the table; sometimes more slowly and at other times more rapidly.
Our bodies would move from side to side; a dance with a table between
us. Jerry and I could even play in the dark and keep that little white ball
going! In my twenties, I played squash with Dick. We played day after
day and it really did not matter who won. We were together in a little
white room encountering each other, influencing each other, creating a
rhythm together. In my thirties, tennis and racquetball captivated me. I
knew with whom I enjoyed playing and with whom I did not, and why.
The essential ingredient is rhythm in relationships, active, communal
sharing. I am reminded of the time when, after several years of jogging
by myself, a neighbor invited me to jog with him. I reluctantly consented
to do so. To my surprise, I enjoyed immensely our synchronized pace and
conversation. I was also struck by how unaware I was of my usual bodily
discomfort. That rhythm kept me afloat!

There is another area in which my sharing of rhythms with another
person has been a compelling experience. In the course of raising my two
small daughters, I have discovered deeply satisfying rhythms. When, as
infants, they had not yet acquired language, I found myself relating their
expressions of sound and movement to my own. I find that with adults
I am mostly aware of communicating with words, ideas, and concepts.
This moves me into a cognitive mode, away from an awareness of the
attraction of movement. With the children, my eyes are always watching;
my body is moving with them. I am alert to the rocking and swaying that
are part of bedtime and bottle feeding. I look back to my sharing of a
drumming session with Rebecka (on her plastic highchair tray) or crawl-

ing in synchrony with Aryn from room to room. They each have their own tempo; their own distinctive motions. The ways in which I mesh rhythmically with each of them reflect unique and significant aspects of my relationship with them. (pp. 3-7)

THE CREATIVE SYNTHESIS

The selected examples of the creative synthesis are from Hawka's unconditional love (1985), Clark's (1988) androgynous male, Snyder's (1988) rejecting love and Vaughn's (1989) writing poetry.

The Experience of Feeling Unconditionally Loved

Hawka (1986) investigated the nature, meaning, and essence of feeling unconditionally loved. From her organization and analysis of data she derived the essential components of the experience. Acceptance, freedom and openness, and energy and power were the key thematic elements that embraced her own experience and that of her co-researchers. In the excerpt which follows, Hawka presents the creative synthesis derived from her composite depiction and portraits of what it means to feel unconditionally loved.

As I consider the experience, an image of ocean waves cascading one upon another comes to me. It is as if the inner world of a person swells to peaks as does the ocean as it rises to a cresting point. Waves of freedom and energy spill over. A flooding with personal love, acceptable and natural, peaceful and relieving, replenishes the empty, dry shell of the personality. As life is restored, vital energies are regenerated and begin to pour out, rising and rushing to reach out to others.

The image of sunlight is also graphically expressive of the feeling of unconditional love. The radiating sun warms the cold, sterile heart of a fearful person. Like the flower, hesitantly, slowly, gently, the person responds with an openness to receive the warmth. The loved person senses the warmth and light suffusing his or her being. Waves of joy, peace, contentment, distinctiveness and lightness of being are all taken in. As this happens, there is a mirroring of these same positive feelings towards others.

Acceptance—The acceptance felt in the experience of unconditional love refers to the affirmation of one's being. Participants felt recognized, acknowledged, respected, welcomed without the imposition of conditions, demands, obligations, responsibilities. In the past, these requirements obscured the fact of one's own being as fundamentally sufficient, adequate, acceptable. In feeling unconditionally loved, individuals are given permission to experience their very being in itself, as good and of value, unconnected and apart from anyone or any functional purpose. Hence, a person receives a clear, undiluted message of love.

Freedom-openness—As soon as the individual experiences the awareness or insight of self-worth, a sense of freedom and an openness ensues. It is like a striking breakthrough, the "eureka" experience, a bright light, a peak moment. The release and relief spread rapidly throughout an individual's being. Old blocks and patterns are shed. Chains, almost on a physical level, are loosened, unlocked, disposed. A feeling of lightness envelops the person, suggesting the real possibility of soaring through the air. New vistas are revealed. Old emotional burdens are surmounted. Captives' potentials are suddenly released and are free to explore and create dreams of being and becoming.

Energy and self-power—This last component refers to the effects that unconditional love had upon its recipients, how it strengthened them in confidence, in trusting themselves, in gaining courage to be. Energy sources hitherto neglected or unknown were revealed. Unconditional love not only pointed to new meanings and life goals, but also disclosed untapped inner resources for pursuing creative pathways.

Finally, it is important to highlight the *dynamic flowing* that connects these components. Taken as a whole, they represent a passage from a burdened and restrained existence to an open and unfettered one; from a deadening past to a vitalizing present and promising future; from a constricted, rigid way of life to a spontaneous process of movement toward self-actualization; from isolation to healthy and satisfying relationships; from an externally controlled self to an inner directed and loving self.

Feeling unconditionally loved is a gift and a challenge. It can be incorporated into one's own being, offering hope and promise for a new life, a raison d'etre for living, a challenge for discovering the hidden qualities of creation that will extend and enrich one's destiny. (pp. 91-93)

Rejecting Love

Snyder's creative synthesis of the essence of rejecting love is as follows:

We cry out silently not asking for the acceptance and unconditional love that we desperately desire. Or we shout in anger at the offering of conditional love that disturbs us and that we don't want. We are confused and cautious. . . .

We may withdraw into a sullen, snarling, protective shell that makes reaching out a near impossibility. When we do reach out, with each reaching we feel more vulnerable. The offering is repulsed with increased intensity, sullenness, and anger. At the same time we continue to want yet we don't want. A quiet peacefulness settles in as the attempts to reach us subside or stop. Like a cornered or wounded animal we relax our guard, but we keep a watchful eye on the surroundings. We go within for nurture and solace. If "they" would only just "be" with us, not "do" anything. This would reveal an understanding. We allow this kind of being to seep ever so slowly into our vast need. Long ago we ceased to ask yet deep down there is still the hunger for unconditional acceptance and love. . . . The internal desire for connectedness persists in spite of many painful doubts and many experiences of rejecting love. . . .

It is though we have been given cold lumpy mashed potatoes and told that it is really a rich creamy vanilla ice cream. But it always turns out to be what it is, cold, empty, weak, conditional, lifeless. In especially hungering and needy times, we may believe in its fullness, in its "no strings attached." But the doubt returns tenfold and within us develops a drivenness to find a love that is pure. At some point, we become the fortunate ones. Each of us, co-researchers and dreamers of the hope of unconditional love, meets someone who accepts us completely and within us awakens the cleansing purity of acceptance and love that makes no demands and imposes no expectations. Then it is not a dream. It is not a fantasy. We experience the full nature, meaning, and essence of unconditional love. Once we experience love in this way, the conditional love loses its attractiveness forever, needy or not. Through receiving unconditional love, we recognize its qualities. We survived in conditional love but we will never accept it again as a substitute once we know the full and unfettered awakening of unconditional love. (pp. 138-141)

The Androgynous Male

Returning to Clark's (1988) investigation of the experience of the psychologically androgynous male, the following presents excerpts from the creative synthesis.

I have sought a synthesis which expresses . . . holistic harmony and balancing of polarities, but also fully captures the dynamic growth and change process in which these men are engaged. . . . a strong image came to me. It was a divining rod—the three-pronged, Y-shaped branch of hazelwood which many have claimed can direct them to underground sources of water. I knew immediately that this was an evocative symbol of my experience of psychological androgyny, and the experiences of the co-researchers.

One branch—the male aspect of self—meets the other—the female aspect —and they join to become one: the guiding or pointing branch, androgyny. Remove any one of the three branches and the divining rod becomes useless. They are all equally important. The rod is a tool, a tool used in the process of discovery. The guiding or pointing part of the rod—the androgynous way of being—is usually depicted as the longest branch of the rod, the part that goes out ahead, seeking discovery. It needs both the male and female to do its work, and they need it to attach and balance them. The male and female are the handles, the grounding or foundation of the rod. The androgynous branch grows out of them and extends their reach, making them useful, giving them purpose.

Given animation by a human being, the divining rod moves, in a continuous process of discovery . . . its symbolic meaning parallels the androgyny process: the balance and unification of the male and female into one whole and harmonious entity, capable of more than each alone, creating more than the sum of its parts. The divining rod is the discoverer of the essence of life . . . and symbolizes our ultimate unity with each other and our world. . . . The experience of androgyny is this never-ending process. It is accepting and trusting the wisdom of the eternal male and the eternal female in balance within one entity, the interplay of achievement and nurture, of doing and being, of separation and attachment, of will and surrender, of aggressivity and passivity, of dominance and compliance, of hardness and softness, of competitiveness and cooperativeness, of logic and emotion, of linear thinking and holistic thinking, of rationalism and intuition, of self-orientation and family-community-global orientation. (pp. 150-154)

The Experience of Writing Poetry

Lynn Vaughn's (1989) study of the experience of writing poetry began with a discovery that some of her own most painful and most joyous experiences were inexpressible in any other form. She found the lyric poem, the song of the soul, the most immediate resource for creative self-expression. Following her own immersion and attunement to writing poetry, she obtained first-person depictions of the experience from 13 volunteer participants. From her data, she constructed portraits, a compositive depiction, and a creative synthesis of the meanings and essences of the experience. The creative synthesis follows:

Sometimes light tries to bend around an object, like a tree or the silhouette of a rock tower, and a sun-star forms at precisely the place where the light comes out of hiding. Writing poetry is like such "god beams," and the crepuscular rays that burst out of an enclosure of clouds when dust particles, or a particular kind of haze, are present.

Being a poet is a vocation, a calling. At any moment a train's whistle, the creaking of two trees rubbing against each other, the sight of pain on a loved one's face may call the poet into the mysterious and timeless world of creating a poem. Awe beckons the poet from important tasks and engrossing conversations, teasing him or her with flashes of color or connectedness, or dazzling sun-stars.

It is a wondrous activity, this chasing after the amorphous and ethereal shadows of truth that call to the writer from behind whatever image or object has captivated his or her attention. The poets who were interviewed for this study used metaphors to convey some of what cannot be said directly, but must be danced around to gain an understanding of what it means to write poetry. . . . The poem is a moment of birth—waves of letting go, of pushing out, the ecstatic pinnacle of emergence and creation. We poets dance around the ineffable, holding hands with the intangible. As in the experience of actually dancing, the poet moves beyond a purely physical sphere and enters into sounds within, into a communion of passion, rhythm and melody. . . . The experience of writing poetry is like being drawn into the vortex of a cloud which opens funnel-like into the spirit world.

Writing poetry is an encounter with mystery. It is an experience of living in the present moment, turning over rocks, diving into emptiness, facing insecurities, knowing special moments of connection with a loved one or with a nightfall cloaked in brilliant blue earth-shadow and wearing a halo of roses. It is an experience of diaphanous filmy scarves moving gracefully, beckoning one into the company of gods and goddesses. It is an awe-filled departure from the everyday in to the sacred, an experience of embracing polarities, of dissolving edges which meld life, energy, purpose, direction, and fulfillment into one design.

Writing poetry is a way of looking into darkness and seeing what cannot be seen. It is a way of listening in the silence, for what cannot be heard, of experiencing both the emptiness and the fullness of all that cannot be held in one's hands. (pp. 81-83)

CLOSING COMMENTS

The power of heuristics is in its recognition of the significance of self-searching and the value of personal knowledge as essential requirements for the understanding of common human experiences. There is no substitute for direct, comprehensive, accurate first-person accounts of experience, for the importance of self-inquiry and self-dialogue in discovering the nature and meaning of one's own experience and that of others. As the distinctiveness of experience is explicated into its unique qualities and themes and depicted through description, example, literary expression, narrative, and artwork, the researcher has gathered what is required to construct the universal portrayal or essence. The researcher intuitively and reflectively sees in all the depictions the qualities or characteristic meanings that make the experience what it is and not something else—what enables one to know anger as anger, tranquility as tranquility, fear as fear, and courage as courage. The creative synthesis is the peak moment when the researcher recognizes the universal nature of what something is and means, and at the same time grows in self-understanding and as a self.

5

Applications of Heuristic Research

LONELINESS—UNRAVELING ITS
NATURE AND MEANING[1]

My interest in loneliness began at a critical time in my life when I was faced with the problem of whether or not to agree to major heart surgery that might restore my daughter to health or result in her death (Moustakas, 1961). I did not consciously set out to study loneliness. I had no research design or hypotheses or assumptions. The urgency of making a critical decision plunged me into the experience of feeling utterly alone, and pushed me to deliberately cut myself off from the advice or guidance of others. The entire process of facing the terror and potential consequence of this life-or-death decision initiated a search into my own self, an engagement of disturbing inner contact in which I tried to be fully aware and discover the right way to proceed. The probing increased my sense of isolation and took me on many lonely paths, each of which ended in a question mark.

Lonely self-reflection came at unexpected moments, in the midst of crowds of people, in response to words or phrases in conversation. Many different kinds of situations evoked an inner process of doubt and uncertainty, and a strong feeling of being isolated and alone. Sometimes I awakened in the night, overwhelmed by images and feelings and thoughts. I tried to draw from myself a single answer that would utilize the significant data that came from conversations with my daughter, talks with physicians, and published reports on heart surgery. Thus the initial journey into loneliness was an attempt to discover a way to proceed: it involved a process of self-inquiry, which was not planned or carefully sampled but which occurred spontaneously at unexpected times and places. Although no clear answer came to the problem of surgery, I became aware that at the center of my world was a deep and pervasive feeling of loneliness.

With this feeling came the realization that loneliness is a capacity or source for new searching, awareness, and inspiration—that when the outside world ceases to have a meaning, when support and confirmation are lacking or are not adequate to assuage human suffering, when doubt and uncertainty overwhelm a person, then the individual may contemplate life from the depths of the self and in nature. For me, this discovery meant that in a crucial and compelling crisis, in spite of comfort and sympathy from others, one can feel utterly and completely alone. At bottom, the experience of loneliness exists in its own right as a source of both pain and power, as a source of darkness and light. I came to see that loneliness is an inevitable experience of life itself.

Thus the beginning steps of my research into loneliness involved not a question of the *nature* of loneliness, or its restorative, creative, or destructive impact on the person, but a struggle and search into another problem—the question of a life-and-death decision regarding another human being (Moustakas, 1967). Much later I realized that loneliness is often experienced by individuals who make crucial decisions that will have major consequences in the lives of others. Through inner exploration and study, I sought to find a solution that would integrate the facts into one clear pattern. The significance of inner searching for deeper awareness is cogently expressed by Michael Polanyi (1964) in his book *Science, Faith and Society*:

> Every interpretation of nature, whether scientific, non-scientific or anti-scientific, is based on some intuitive conception of the general nature of things. . . . But in spite of much beautiful work . . . we still have no clear conception of how discovery comes about. The main difficulty has been pointed out by Plato in the *Meno*. He says that to search for the solution of a problem is an absurdity. For either you know what you are looking for, and then there is no problem; or you do not know what you are looking for, and then you are not looking for anything and cannot expect to find anything. . . . A potential discovery may be thought to attract the mind which will reveal it—inflaming the scientist with creative desire and imparting to him intimations that guide him from clue to clue and from surmise to surmise. The testing hand, the straining eye, the ransacked brain, may all be thought to be labouring under the common spell of a potential discovery striving to emerge into actuality. (pp. 10-14)

Experiences in meditation and self-searching, intuitive and mystical reachings, and hours of silent midnight walking paved the way to a formulation of my understanding of loneliness. This formulation emerged clearly during my observations of hospitalized children. In the hospital I saw how lonely feelings impelled young children to seek a compassionate voice and a warm, friendly face. I saw how young children separated from their parents could often be more completely involved in the struggle with loneliness than in the painful experiences connected with illness and surgery. I observed how these children underwent a period of protest and resistance against separation, against the mechanical actions and fixed faces and gestures of the hospital combine. I also observed a gradual deterioration of protest, rebellion, and self-assertion to be replaced by a deep sense of isolation, lonely weeping, withdrawal, depression, and numbness. In general, I witnessed a basic, pervasive process of dehumanization in an institution that not only sought to repress lonely feelings but discouraged the whole range of human emotions that characterize the alive and growing child.

When I saw that these dimensions of loneliness were almost totally ignored, misunderstood, and rejected by hospital aides, nurses, and doctors, I decided—using the hospital situation and my own intuitive awareness as a beginning—to study the nature of loneliness, how it fitted into the perceptions and behavior of hospitalized children, and the way in which it existed in myself and others. I listened to the experiences of children in the hospital and to their spontaneous expressions of loneliness, keeping the focus of my interest on the essence of the lonely experience through the children's renderings of it. I wanted to know the truth of loneliness in its most basic, objective forms.

Objectivity, in this connection, means seeing what an experience *is* for another person—not its cause, its reason for existence, nor its definition and classification. It means seeing attitudes, beliefs, and feelings of the person as they exist at the moment, perceiving them whole, as a unity. I set out to know the meaning of loneliness, not by defining and categorizing it but by experiencing it directly myself and through the lives of others, as a simple reality of life. George E. Moore (1959) describes this kind of reality in *Principia Ethica*:

My point is that "good" is a simple notion, just as "yellow" is a simple notion, that, just as you cannot, by any manner of means, explain to anyone who does not already know it, what yellow is, so you cannot explain what good is. Definitions of the kind that I was asking for, definitions which describe the real nature of the object or notion denoted by a word, and which do not merely tell us what the word is used to mean, are only possible when the object or notion in question is something complex. You can give a definition to a horse, because a horse has many different properties and qualities, all of which you can enumerate. But when you have enumerated them all, when you have reduced a horse to his simplest terms, then you can no longer define those terms. They are simply something which you think of or perceive, and to any one who cannot think of or perceive them, you can never, by any definition, make their nature known.

I set out to discover the meaning of loneliness in its simplest terms and in its native state. I knew from my own experiences and from my conversations with hospitalized children that loneliness itself could not be communicated by words or defined in its essence, or appreciated and recognized except by persons who are open to their own senses and aware of their own experiences. I set out to discover the nature of lonely experience by intimate encounter with other persons. A quotation from Polanyi's *Personal Knowledge* (1962) further clarifies this point:

> To say that the discovery of objective truth in science consists in the apprehension of a rationality which commands our respect and arouses our contemplative admiration; that such discovery, while using the experience of our senses as clues, transcends this experience by embracing the vision of a reality beyond the impression of our senses, a vision which speaks for itself in guiding us to an ever deeper understanding of reality—such an account of scientific procedure would be generally shrugged aside as out-dated Platonism; a piece of mystery-mongering unworthy of an enlightened age. Yet it is precisely on this conception of objectivity that I wish to insist. . . . Into every act of knowing there enters a passionate contribution of the person knowing what is known, and . . . this coefficient is no mere imperfection but a vital component of his knowledge.

Initially, I studied loneliness in its essential forms by putting myself into an open, ready state, into the lonely experiences of hospitalized children, and letting these experiences become the focus of my world. I listened. I watched. I stood by. In dialogue with the children, I tried to put into words the depth of their feelings. Sometimes my words touched a child and tears began to flow; sometimes the child formed words in response to my presence, and broke through the numbness and the dehumanizing impact of the hospital atmosphere and practice. In a strong sense, loneliness became my existence. It entered into every facet of my world—into my teaching, my interviews in therapy, my conversations with friends, my home life. Without reference to time or place or structure, somehow (more intentionally than accidentally) the loneliness theme came up everywhere in my life. At this time, I became clearly aware that, exhaustively and fully and in a caring way, I was searching for, studying, and inquiring into the nature and impact of loneliness. I was totally immersed in the search for a pattern that would reveal the various dimensions of loneliness. I was closely searching and inquiring into the nature of a human experience, not from a detached intellectual or academic position, but rooted in its integrative, living forms. I became part of the lonely experience of others, involved and interested, while at the same time aware of enlarging themes and patterns. Facts and knowledge accumulated as I listened and later recorded and studied them; but, at the same time, there were intuitive visions, feelings, and sensings that went beyond anything I could record or know in a factual sense. At the center of each lonely existence were ineffable, indescribable feelings and experiences, which I felt in a unified and essential way. I had, at moments, gone "wide open"—ceasing to be a separate individual, but wholly related to the other person, leaving something behind of my own intuitive vision and comprehension while at the same time taking something away—very much in the manner of Steinbeck and Ricketts (1941) in their study of the *Sea of Cortez*:

> Let's see what we see, record what we find, and not only fool ourselves with conventional scientific strictures—in that lonely and uninhabited Gulf our boat and ourselves would change it the moment we entered. By going there, we would bring a new factor to the Gulf. Let us consider that factor and not be betrayed by this myth of permanent objective reality. If it exists at all it is only available in pickled tatters or in distorted flashes. "Let us go," we said, "into the Sea of Cortez, realizing that we become forever a part of it; that our rubber boots slogging through a flat of eelgrass, that the rocks we turn over in a tide pool, make us truly and permanently a factor in the ecology of the region. We shall take something away from it, but we shall leave something too." (p. 3)

In a similar way, I began a formal study of loneliness, combining my own growing self-awareness and discovery of myself as a lonely person with my experiences in the hospital, and conversations and discussions with other persons—children in school settings, who spoke freely and openly and wrote themes expressing their lonely experiences; parents and young adults in therapy, who initially found it painful to speak of loneliness but were soon able to recapture and create in a living sense moments of the past and current feelings of isolation and solitude; and friends and colleagues, who revealed in intimate terms the impact of the loneliness experience. I steeped myself in a world of loneliness, letting my life take root and unfold in it, letting its dimensions and meanings and forms evolve in its own timetable and dynamics and ways.

The study culminated in my readings of published reports on loneliness and lonely experiences. But this was a point near the end, not at the beginning where it might have acted to predispose or color my own growing awareness. I studied biographies and autobiographies of individuals who dramatically exemplified lonely lives: Emily Dickinson (1927; Chase, 1951), Abraham Lincoln (Herndon & Weik, 1920), Woodrow Wilson (Day, 1952), and Benedict Arnold and Ned Langford (Burgess, 1940). I followed the lonely experiences of Herman Buhl (1956) in his journey to the highest peak of the Himalayas, Admiral Byrd (1938) on an advanced base in Antarctica, Saint Exupery (1939, 1957) lost in the desert, and other persons involved in extreme situations of isolation (Burgess, 1940; Thoreau, 1955). To understand more fully the lonely consequences of infamy and mass public rejection, I studied the autobiographical volumes of Alger Hiss (1957) and Whitaker Chambers (1952) as well as political analyses of their trial and its implications, including the volumes of the House Un-American Activities Committee and the 10 volumes of the trial transcript.

I discovered additional nuances of the meaning of loneliness from the studies of Frieda Fromm-Reichmann (1959) of the loneliness of mental patients; Margaret Wood's *Paths of Loneliness* (1953); Eithne Tabor's *The Cliff's Edge: Songs of a Psychotic* (1950); Karl Menninger's *Love Against Hate* (1942); David Riesman's *The Lonely Crowd* (1950); Erich Fromm's *Escape From Freedom* (1941); Thomas Wolfe's *Hills Beyond* (1941); Sullivan's *Interpersonal Theory of Psychiatry* (1953); and Robertson's *Young Children in Hospitals* (1959). The numerous articles and reports appearing in newspapers and journals also received my attention. These accounts could be interpreted as attempts to overcome loneliness and as evolutions of deeper sensitivity and awareness that enabled unique and creative expressions of loneliness in poetry, music, literature, and other art forms.

When a pattern began to emerge with reference to the nature and function of loneliness in individual experience and in modern living, the formal study came to an end. At this point the framework and the clarification of loneliness had been established. It was now possible to differentiate and refine the meaning of loneliness, to expand and illustrate its nature and relevance in human experience. Thus what started as a hospital study of loneliness became an extended search into the phenomenon of loneliness.

The chain of conditions and factors that initiated and characterized the study were: (1) a crisis, which created a question or problem; (2) a search of self in solitude, from which emerged a recognition of the significance of loneliness both as a creative urging and as a frightening and disturbing experience; (3) an expanding awareness through being open to lonely life and lonely experiences, through watching, listening, feeling, and through conversation, dialogue, and discussion; (4) a steeping of myself in the deeper regions of loneliness, so that it became the center of my world; (5) an intuitive/factual grasping of the patterns of loneliness, and related aspects and different associations, until an integrated vision and awareness emerged; (6) further clarification, delineation, and refinement through studies of lonely lives, lonely experiences, and published reports on loneliness; and (7) creation of a manuscript in which to project and express the various forms, themes, and values of loneliness and to present its creative powers, as well as the anxiety it arouses in discontent, restlessness, and boredom, and the strategies used in attempting to overcome and escape loneliness.

My studies awakened me to the creative power of loneliness, and the resources it offers in the process of searching and studying. I saw the value of being open to significant dimensions of experience in which comprehension and compassion mingle; intellect, emotion, and spirit are integrated; and intuition, spontaneity, and self-exploration are seen as components of unified experience.

Since the publication of *Loneliness*, I have received approximately 2,000 letters that validate my portrayal of the nature of loneliness in modern life. My correspondents confirmed the meaning and essence of loneliness as congruent with the depictions that had emerged from my research. These persons portrayed the uniqueness of lonely experience and its powers in drawing upon untouched capacities and resources, in evolving new creations, and expanding awareness, sensitivity, and compassion. They revealed also the extreme pain, grief, despair, and impotency that often accompany the urge to discover, or the suffering involved in answering challenges and problems of living. They represented an opportunity for the readers to talk back to an author, to say for themselves how loneliness touched their lives, and what it expressed in the way of creation. The fear of self-discovery is a strong component in avoiding loneliness and solitude. Once this courageous step is taken there is no turning back.

The focus of my research has been a study of loneliness. I now believe in a heuristic process of searching and studying, of being open to significant dimensions of experience, and pursuing knowledge through self-inquiry, full immersion into the phenomenon, and spontaneous observation of and dialogue with persons who are experiencing the phenomenon. A passage from an essay of Carl Rogers (1965) points to the values of a heuristic process:

> In the first place it would tend to do away with the fear of creative subjective speculation. As I talk with graduate students in the behavioral sciences, this fear is a very deep one. It cuts them off from any significant discovery. They would be shocked by the writings of a Kepler in his mystical and fanciful searchings for likenesses and patterns in nature. They do not recognize that it is out of such fanciful thinking that true science emerges. . . .

> A second effect would be to place a stress on disciplined commitment, disciplined *personal* commitment, not methodology. It would be a very healthy emphasis in the behavioral sciences if we could recognize that it is the dedicated, personal search of a disciplined, open-minded individual which discovers and creates new knowledge. No refinement of laboratory or statistical method can do this. . . .

> Another effect would be that it would permit a free rein to phenomenological thinking in behavioral science, our effort to understand man and perhaps even the animals from the inside. It would recognize that no type of hypothesis has any special virtue in science save only in its relationship to a meaningful pattern which exists in the universe. . . .

> Another and more general effect would be that if the picture of science I have tried to suggest gains some general acceptance in our field then it

would give a new dignity to the science of man and to the scientist who commits himself to that field. It would keep the scientist as a human being in the picture at all times, and we would recognize that science is but the lengthened shadow of dedicated human beings. (pp. 192-193)

THE SYMBOLIC GROWTH EXPERIENCE AND HEURISTIC RESEARCH

An important application of heuristic research has been its contribution as a process of discovery in investigations of the symbolic growth experience (SGE). Symbolic growth refers to a sudden, dramatic shift in perception, belief, or understanding that alters one's frame of reference or world view. The internal change or revision is usually connected with an external event but the connection is synchronistic, an intentional or spontaneous happening rather than the result of a cause-effect relationship. The shift in perception and meaning launches in some measure a new attitude, a new process of learning, a character or personality shift in identity and selfhood.

Over a period of many years, Willard Frick (1983, 1987a, 1987b, 1990) has been a pioneer researcher in studies of the symbolic growth experience. His investigations have been rooted in heuristic processes of discovery of the nature, meaning, essence and implications of the symbolic growth experience.

Frick's recognition of the importance of the symbolic growth experience was launched during his reading of Carson McCuller's *The Heart is a Lonely Hunter.* In the process of study and reflection, he became aware of the potential of immediate experience, the value of the symbolic in radically altering one's self-perceptions, self-image and self-concept. From his initial analysis, Frick formulated a core question: Is symbolic growth a potential reality of lived experience? He examined biographies and autobiographies as well as works of fiction that contained material relevant to symbolic growth. He also solicited first-person accounts of the experience. This phase of his research included the heuristic processes of immersion, incubation, and illumination. Through the early stages of his investigation, Frick (1990) collected depictions of the symbolic growth experience and arrived at a beginning clarification of its nature. He defined symbolic growth as *a conscious perception of the symbolic-metaphorical dimension of immediate experience leading to heightened awareness, the creation of meaning, and personal growth* (p. 68).

The next phase of his work was that of heuristic explication of the phenomenon of symbolic growth. Frick explored the experience more fully and more deeply and studied its impact on people's lives. He discovered that the symbolic growth experience served a special purpose in individual development. It was awakened at propitious moments and made a major contribution to the development of the identity of the person. He also came to see that the experience was a special example of synchronicity, a meaningful coincidence in which there was no evidence of a causal relationship between the external event and the internal discovery. Relevant to the learning process, Frick states:

> In all of the SGEs I studied, the individuals created/discovered important meanings out of that experience; meanings that were not objectively represented or inherent in the context or logical structure of the events themselves. I began to believe that the SGE could serve as a model for a new perspective on human learning based on the creation of meaning; on the existential dimension of human experience. (p. 70)

From further analysis of his data, Frick (1990) elucidated two characteristics that represented permeating themes of the symbolic growth experience: (1) *Integration, order,* and *stability* through which the individual attains self-consistency and brings unity and completion to an incomplete structure of personality; and (2) *differentiation, change,* and *growth* through which the individual discovers and actualizes new facets of the self. The symbolic growth experience serves as a bridge to unify these two contradictory forces, enabling "a harmony of purpose and expression in the personality" (p. 71). Frick emphasizes that "the SGE thus becomes a liberating experience for it transcends all of the artificial barriers, disharmony, and distance we have established between ourselves and the substance of our being and existence. A more total reality emerges encompassing both the person and environment" (p. 73).

The SGE also serves a corrective function in initiating a resolution to dysfunctional life routines and habits, patterns that repeat themselves in work, and in relationship to one's own self and others. Frick concluded that the symbolic and conceptual powers of the individual provide a powerful corrective and therapeutic force in the personality.

An example of the corrective power of the SGE is expressed in a shift which occurs in a movement from disappointment and rejection to exhilaration and acceptance (Frick, 1990):

> The most traumatic event in my life was learning that my wife, Barbara, was pregnant. I couldn't face it and wouldn't accept it. The baby was unplanned, unwanted and it all seemed like a cruel joke to me.
>
> Recently out of college, we needed more time to get settled and build some financial security. We also needed more time to develop our relationship. We were both disappointed in the pregnancy, but while Barbara began to develop a real love and anticipation for the baby, I tried to ignore it all. This was relatively easy for me for a while for there were no apparent physical changes.
>
> As changes took place, however, as Barbara gained weight and her abdomen swelled, I became more and more anxious; less and less tolerant for the fact of life. One night, while sleeping close to Barbara, I pressed my body against her warm stomach and felt the baby move. I felt the kicks and rolls against my body. Slowly, I placed my hand against Barbara's belly and began to feel a deep communication with my wife and child. From that moment on I was never the same. The experience of feeling the movement of the fetus against my body was a conversion experience of great impact upon me. I felt a sudden exultation for life and for my capacity to create a human being. I also felt myself taking part in a larger drama of creation and participating in the most fundamental rhythm of mankind: birth and death. I had never before felt such a harmony and oneness with the cosmos.
>
> I experienced a renewed sense of kinship with my family, my parents and grandparents, the long lineage stretching back into darkness. I was very much a part of that history, that continuity of life and identity. In one brief moment of experiencing, lying there with our bodies together; my negative attitude toward my wife's pregnancy ceased. No longer did I ignore or resent our child. An incredible change had taken place within me. It was the most awesome experience I have ever had. (pp. 73-74)

In addition to the corrective shift in the resolution of an issue or problem, the symbolic growth experience launches an enhancement of identity and selfhood. An example of the enhancement function of the SGE illustrates the kind of heuristic data that Frick (1990) has been collecting over a period of years.

An experience that I can remember more clearly than any others took place when I was twelve years old. We were at camp and three friends and I were looking at the stars. It was a clear evening and somebody brought up the scientific fact he had learned that the whole universe, the stars and planets, were all in motion. This thought just struck me. I never thought of the whole universe as in motion before. The more I thought about it, the more it seemed true that everything was moving, changing; the stars, the planets, the wind, the ground, the grass under my feet. It hit me that in this sense, everything was alive and nothing was really inert, never changing, and dead. (p. 76)

In his observations of the relationship between his studies of the symbolic growth experience and heuristic research, theory, concepts and processes, Frick observes that

At the base of all other attributes of heuristic research is the freedom of exploration and inquiry, an assumption of integrity, granted to the investigator. I was not bound, as in more conventional research, by preconceptions or operational definitions, nor was I constrained by hypotheses to prove or disprove. Thus there were few impositions, few artificial strictures, placed on my data. This allowed the essence of the experience to reveal itself over time. It was also this freedom of inquiry that permitted me to draw upon data from a variety of sources including biographical, autobiographical, and fictional materials, and from solicited personal accounts.

No other investigative procedure could have yielded the insights and discoveries that emerged during the course of this study, reaching a climax in the realization of synthesis—the identification of a healing and growth enhancing agency within the personality. In this respect, therefore, this study met the heuristic challenge . . . to generate a new reality a new monolithic significance, that embodies the essence of the heuristic truth." (Douglass & Moustakas, 1985, p. 52, p. 79).

From Frick's work and that of other heuristic researchers, it is clear that heuristic processes and methods offer rich possibilities for understanding transitions in the development of identity, personality, character and selfhood. Heuristic methods also open channels for revisioning motivation and the dynamic processes involved in human learning. They offer guides and methods that can be used in the resolution of dysfunctional behavior, but also in corrections of distorted perceptions and handicapping beliefs. Heuristic processes applied to the symbolic growth experience can lead to enhancement of self-efficacy in decision making and in new creations of life meanings.

PERSON-CENTERED THERAPY AND HEURISTIC INQUIRY

Applications of heuristic research to person-centered therapy were examined by O'Hara (1986) and also by Barrineau and Bozarth (1989) in their studies of human science inquiry and its relationship to psychotherapy. These authors concluded that the core conditions essential to therapeutic personality change formulated by Rogers (1957) were congruent with qualitative research concepts and processes and an adequate basis for heuristic inquiry. O'Hara emphasized that person-centered therapy "is itself, a heuristic investigation into the nature and meaning of human experience. In his work with clients, Rogers discovered that when a person is engaged passionately and skillfully in the search for his or her own truth *the process itself is therapeutic* . . . scientific and therapeutic gains could be made at the same time" (p. 174).

In distinguishing quantitative and qualitative research approaches, Barrineau and Bozarth (1989) point to a key difference; namely "that in heuristic inquiry spontaneous creation of new methods or changing methods in midstream is not only allowed, but is encouraged" (p. 467). Freedom of the researcher or therapist to shift perspectives and methods at any point in the process recognizes the contribution that subjectivity and immediacy make to knowledge. Subjectivity is an essential condition of the real (Douglass & Moustakas, 1985). Rogers (1968) also has observed that in research it is essential that research procedures "keep the scientist as a human being in the picture at all times."

Patton (1990) has made extensive investigations of qualitative methodology especially as related to evaluation studies and outcome research. In his paper on humanistic psychology and humanistic research, Patton observes that qualitative research inquiry attends to the uniqueness of each case, while in humanistic psychology each person is perceived as unique; data collection in qualitative research is individualized—the therapeutic process is also individualized; the humanistic researcher seeks to capture the co-researcher's experience—the humanistic psychotherapist focuses on the client's perspective; both approaches establish direct interpersonal contact, in the one case with the client, in the other with the research participant; therapist and researcher are accepting, caring, and nonjudgmental; and in both approaches there is concern for the whole person. Patton concludes, "The qualitative researcher, in being open and inductive, works from a flexible design. . . . The humanistic psychologist is flexible in responding to client needs and interests" (p. 15). Both are process oriented in studying emerging and unfolding experiences of the client or research participant.

Continuing with their analysis of the relationship between person-centered therapy and heuristic research, no assumptions, expectations, or theoretical interpretations are made by the researcher or therapist. Rather, the person in therapy or the research participant, searching into the nature of an experience, depicts and illustrates the inner world of feelings, thoughts, and meanings that embody and permeate the experience, the core themes that form the textures and structures of critical life events and lead directly to clarification, insight, and restoration of self-hidden meanings. A crucial shift in consciousness occurs. "This view acknowledges healing as a *natural consequence* of a successful moment in a progressive search for truth" (O'Hara, 1986, p. 177).

Barrineau and Bozarth (1989) assert that "the difference between therapy and heuristic research of the person-centered model is a moot one. The model, for therapy, promotes the actualizing tendency. The model, for research, promotes the same process that includes, for the participants, clarity of discourse" (p. 469). These authors distinguish person-centered therapy from heuristic research in terms of therapeutic and research intentions. Throughout, the therapist facilitates the actualizing process while the researcher collects data as the self-searching process unfolds and ultimately collects, codes, and analyzes the data in terms of descriptive meanings, core themes, and creative illustrations and renderings of the research participants' experience.

The therapist's philosophy, state Barrineau and Bozarth, follows the direction and pace of the client while communicating and dialoguing with the client in a genuine way, as a real person, with unconditional valuing of the client and empathic understanding of the client's world. They view these qualities as essential in heuristic inquiry as well. Quoting Douglass and Moustakas (1985), they point to the challenge of heuristic research: "to examine all the collected data in creative combinations and recombinations, sifting and sorting, moving rhythmically in and out of appearance, looking, listening carefully for the meanings within meanings, attempting to identify the overarching qualities that inhere in the data" (p. 472). The discipline and dedication of the investigator is to discover the truth, "rather than external rules and methods of control for objectivity espoused by the scientific method" (p. 472).

These interconnections and interrelationships between person-centered therapy and heuristic research enable a fuller understanding of the discovery process. In both approaches, there is an opening out of internal perceptions, feelings, and meanings, a process of self-development leading to clearer understandings and projections into new experience. Both approaches recognize the significance of the person's frame of reference, internal experience, and the value of indwelling, honesty, authenticity, human presence, and mutuality as catalysts for self-discovery and self-renewal. Both approaches emphasize that their primary concern is the person's unfolding sense of truth, explication of experience to deeper levels of meaning, and expansion of consciousness.

As O'Hara (1986) concludes, "There is substantial evidence that at moments of revelation people move toward psychological health, whether in a religious, scientific, artistic or therapeutic context. This is the only basis for claims that this mutual exploration is, in fact, a valid form of psychotherapy" (p. 183).

HEURISTIC METHODOLOGY APPLIED TO PSYCHOTHERAPY

The heuristic process requires direct and active participation of the therapist seeking to understand the nature and essence of the problem that permeates the other person's world. Such participation involves special moments of self-awareness and an openness to metaphysical forms of knowing. From this point of view, the individual is considered the fundamental agent for identifying and describing the problem. The discovery process, however, draws upon the tacit knowledge and intuitions of both persons (Moustakas, 1981). The private nature and the uniqueness of heuristic therapy invites mutual trust in internal processes of self-searching and self-dialogue. Living inside a therapeutic relationship opens avenues of knowing that are not possible through formal or external operations.

Throughout, the therapist and person in therapy move through various phases of the heuristic process. From the beginning an atmosphere is created for mutual discovery. Important connections are made that open pathways to resolution. The heuristic therapist discerns what is of substance in the other's world, focuses on that, and assists the other person in explicating the meanings connected with it.

To be engaged fully in therapy in a heuristic sense means to enter into a relationship with the intention of understanding the essence of the other's experience. This kind of process awakens new images, meanings, and realizations. The studies of hallucination by van Dusen (1973) vividly exemplify this type of heuristic approach. After dealing with hundreds of diagnosed psychotic patients, he discovered that it was possible to speak to their hallucinations. Although the voices that his patients heard were at times frightened of van Dusen he stayed with them; he reassured them and got inside them until they accepted him and he could hear the essence of what they heard. Ultimately he held conversations with the voices, and was able to distinguish the higher order from lower order hallucinations. The voices told him that lower order hallucinations exist to reveal the weaknesses of a person; they threaten, cajole, and ridicule. The higher voices bring out the gifts of creation; they shed light; they inspire; and they are genuinely supportive. These meanings were discovered by van Dusen through his own internal processes of encounter and dialogue with visions, sounds, images, and symbols. The voices of hallucination spoke to him, called to him, and moved him in a way that he was able to enter their lower and higher states. He befriended them and communicated with them comfortably. He was at home with them. Ultimately, this enabled him to help his patients find new ways of being.

Heuristic psychotherapy is like a dance creation, a combination of verbal and bodily expressions that reaches a significant level of mutuality and communion between the therapist and the person in therapy. A rhythm and flow are established that make communication at the deepest levels possible. A mutuality of identities, compassion, and empathy facilitates the heuristic processes of psychotherapy.

From the opening moments with this other person, I, as the therapist, immerse myself in his or her world. I become totally absorbed, curious, alert, and open, ready to enter into each expression. I want to understand what this person is expressing not only from his or her frame of reference, but from the vantage point of my own experience. Eventually what is expressed by the other person mingles with my own knowledge and experience. The meaning that is derived is intersubjective. My understanding of the experience is not an exact copy, but there is a mutuality of meaning that connects us in our awareness and understanding. I steep myself into his or her words, silence, actions, and creations, and understand his or her meanings. My energy, thoughts, and feelings, my self is centered in the other person's life. Gradually, but definitely, we connect in knowledge, understanding, and experience. Through heuristic methods, I come to know the other person's world within the context of my own life.

The first phase of heuristic psychotherapy involves just this process of engaging the other, creating a climate of freedom and openness and preparing for mutual discoveries of meaning. The preliminary encounters enable the other person and me to see the overriding concerns, themes, issues, or problems that are plaguing his or her life and creating a chronic darkness. From these "data," the central theme or problem is identified. The challenge of heuristic therapy is to aim for a wide-open entrance into the other's experience, to search into and explore the overriding problem—when it arises, how, what precipitates it, who is involved, what feelings and thoughts accompany it, and what activities aim at circumventing the problem or resolving it.

In the initial engagement, not only is a climate of freedom and openness created and the theme or problem of focus determined, but there is a gradual but definite relationship—an intersubjectivity and mutuality—that is being formed. Such a relationship involves a rhythmic flow of dialogue and communion, one that increasingly creates an intimate bond and unity between the therapist and the person in therapy. Rogers (1989) describes this kind of relationship in his conversation with Martin Buber:

> I feel that when I'm being effective as a therapist . . . I am relatively whole in that relationship, or the word that has meaning to me is transparent. To be sure there may be many aspects of my life that aren't brought into the relationship, but what is brought into the relationship is transparent. There is nothing hidden. Then I think, too, that in such a relationship I feel a real willingness for this other person to *be what he is.* . . . I think in those moments I am able to sense, with a good deal of clarity, the way his experience seems to him, really viewing it from within him, and yet without losing my own personhood or separateness in that. Then, if in addition to those things on *my* part, my client or the person with whom

I'm working is able to sense something of those attitudes in me, then it seems to me that there is a real, experiential meeting of persons, in which each of us is changed. (p. 48)

The initial engagement in heuristic psychotherapy is the essential first step. Its nature is conveyed in Joan Snyder's account (1983) of her first meeting with Walt, a patient:

Walt came in, stood awhile, began to talk about the side effects of the drugs he had taken. He described his blurred vision. I was aware that his stance communicated a panicky state, and my inner response was to want to reassure him like a little boy protesting the darkness. I wanted to hold him and comfort him. I felt this would not be understood at this point in our relationship, but I encouraged him a second time to be comfortable and sit down. He did. Words tumbled out of his mouth. "I'm supposed to be the breadwinner, and take care of my family. I've always been a good worker. My boss counted on me to go the extra mile. I feel like I'm a failure. I don't know what to do. I used to think I was all alone in this, but I know there are others unemployed like me. When I get my unemployment check everyone else looks like they're getting along o.k. Probably some of them feel like me . . . afraid." "Afraid?" I asked. "Yes, I feel a shaking in my stomach, a quivering, then it moves up to here." His fingers pointed to his breast bone near his heart. "Sometimes in the morning, I think and think with this shaking. 'I've got to do something quick, get a skill. If I take a $5.00 an hour job, I'll lose everything.' . . . I worry something will stop working and there will be extra expense for repairs. I feel as if I'm stuck in a corner and don't know how to get out." He was holding his hands tight together and his arms and left shoulder twitched. I was there with him in his immobility. He continued to talk. "My mother was divorced when I was three, and she and I went to live with her mother. I've seen my father only twice since. I don't care if I ever see him. . . . My mother married again when I was five and my stepfather has been like a father to me. I was always treated equal." This . . . echoed in my mind the next twenty four hours.

I was a child of divorced parents also. I moved to live with my maternal grandparents. They treated me as an equal, but I did not feel an equal. Tears spilled out of my eyes. Ah, Walt, I felt discarded by my parents, too, banished, different from all the other children who lived with their mothers and fathers. I wondered about Walt. How was it for him to have stepbrothers and sisters? I immersed myself in my own unequalness. I felt how he may have felt. I remembered his standing, his tightly clenched hands, and the twitch of his arms. An immobile stance. My own immobility as I, too, experienced fear at seven and a half. "What can I do? What will happen to me? I must hide my feelings as much as I can . . . be strong . . . do what grandma says . . . please the grownups . . . choose a path of adequate performance, be a good girl, a success. Be a success in the ways I think they want . . . quiet behavior . . . reading . . . scholastic achiever . . . not moving, dancing, in my own style. Ah, Walt . . . you, too, chose an adapted path. It worked for many years, and now it isn't working.

The initial engagement of the therapist and the person in therapy is followed by the process of *immersion,* which creates a sense of mutuality and communion between them. The intensity and fullness of these phases are so compelling that a distraction or period of rest is required. It is the process of *incubation* that makes possible the deeper understanding or illumination—the sudden insight or realization that comes when one is not laboring for it—a full, clear understanding that is growing within. To truly know this person in the stirrings and deepenings of heart and mind, the therapist must not pressure, direct, or control, but rather must wait and permit awarenesses and meanings to generate in their own time. The therapist must permit glimmerings and awakenings to form between self and other, allow the birth of understanding to take place in its own readiness and completeness, so that it fits the moment and facilitates new energy and life. Such a process makes possible discovery of new resources and meanings in the relationship.

Immersion and incubation are essential phases in the growth process. In heuristic therapy, there are ways of permitting life to unfold, allowing *what is* to be explored in its own way, until a healthy realization is achieved that moves the person in therapy to new understandings, determinations, and actions.

At some point in the immersion phase it is necessary to stop being absorbed in the problem, to move away from it into another world; enter other activities, wander off to other things. Even a few moments of quiet withdrawal help to restore one's gaze, concentration, and awareness. In a sense the withdrawal is not detachment from the problem, for there is still inside a warming up to the issue, a brooding over it, a sense of being connected to it until a crucial insight becomes strong enough to be born.

Bill put it this way: "I'm coming to therapy because my teacher says I have a problem. I'm a hyperactive child!" But what does it mean to be hyperactive? As Bill put it, it means having "wild, powerful animals inside me that are screaming to get out. I have to keep moving." So move he did—into ferocious rhythms and exaggerated jumps and leaps until all the wild animals were out roaming. Then, until they returned inside him, he could sit quietly, draw, work, read, or play in his own way. He could incubate the wild creatures only so long, and then they would have to get out.

In the incubation process we are rooted in something; it lingers inside until it breaks out into the open as a revolution of thought or feeling—a new idea, a startling revelation, a perspective, or an illumination. It becomes strong enough and courageous enough to come into consciousness and find a way to expression.

Closely related to immersion is another heuristic method known as *indwelling*. Immersion enables one to grasp the whole, to enter completely into all facets of it. Indwelling is an internal process of thinking and feeling into deeper and deeper levels of a person's expressions and behaviors. Through immersion, I obtain knowledge of the person in his or her world. By dwelling inside this knowledge, I obtain refinements, deeper meanings, additional nuances, flavors, and textures—thus I am coming to know this other human being at a level of depth and comprehension that is entirely new, full, and satisfying. Indwelling enables me to mingle freely in internal searches for meaning, to entertain thoughts and feelings, and to incorporate or discard them depending on the fit. I dwell inside my experience with a person to understand the essential parameters of my knowledge. Ultimately, I derive a complete picture of the person—the essential constituents of his or her desires, interests, hopes, fears, self-perceptions, and disappointments; all of the parameters of self-concept and self-attitude and their relationship to the issue or problem that is creating conflict and misery in this person's life.

This phase of therapy might be regarded as the period of *illumination*. Out of the initial engagement and immersion in the person's world, I discover the parameters that are critical, the major structures or themes, and the horizons of his or her experience. I then enter a process of indwelling to explore each of the themes, move easily among the different facets of the person's world, and come to know them in the context of the person's way of being. Illumination involves a period of dwelling inside each structure to obtain a deeper level of awareness and meaning.

Of course, in my interaction with this person, I must check out my knowledge. In doing this, I employ an *internal frame of reference*. I ask the person to consider my understanding and how it fits with his or her own experience. In the interchange, I have an opportunity to help the person or myself recognize, clarify, elaborate on and correct awarenesses and meanings regarding his or her attitudes and behavior. The internal frame of reference puts knowledge back where it belongs, in the perceptions and experiences of the knower. My usual experience when my knowledge is based on heuristic processes is that the person confirms my portrayal—not only confirms, but actually supports it. This is not surprising, because what I see and hear and come to know in the first place is based on what this person has expressed silently and in words and actions.

The internal frame of reference offers an opportunity to verbalize knowledge, to bring meanings and awarenesses out into the open so that they can be used as bases for further exploration and action. The disclosures, as such, are of considerable importance in the developing relationship; the focus on recognition of and attention to the person reinforces the therapist's interest in and concern for him or her. What is more satisfying than knowing that one's own understanding and knowledge of one's self, in the most intimate and profound meanings, is also now in the awareness of another human being? This process of coming to be known through the internal frame of reference and through dialogues between the therapist and the person in therapy facilitates a breakthrough in therapeutic relations. It often represents the first time in a person's life that being understood is complete, and is consistent with one's own understanding.

Recognition of the internal frame of reference enables a person to communicate with greater freedom to reveal previously hidden or guarded perceptions. As a therapist I verbalize the knowledge I have obtained through immersion and indwelling, and the person verifies, elaborates, and corrects it. The respective frames of reference of the person in therapy and the therapist are in harmony. Both knowledges grow out of the actual world of reality and fantasy in which the person in therapy lives; both are based on the same resources, the same internal clues, and the same human conditions.

Another important heuristic method is that of *intuition*. Not all knowledge of the person in therapy comes from indwelling and immersion. Intuitions regarding the meaning of another person's behavior and experience do not come solely from what the person says or does. They grow partly out of the therapist's knowledge of human development, previous experience in a variety of situations, intimations perceived from vague and undifferentiated clues in the person's communications and partly from unknown human sources, tacit knowledge and understanding. Intuitions are hunches, but they are extremely important in therapeutic work—often precipitating a breakthrough in repetitive behaviors, or the breakup of a stalemate in the relationship. Intuitive action may be just what is required to facilitate the next step in a person's growth. Intuitive promptings may be definite or tentative, but when based on solid experience they generally offer a rich potential for new life. As with many hunches, intuitive awarenesses can be checked out without damage to the person in therapy or the relationship.

In almost every relationship, eventually the intuitive component makes the difference between remaining in secure boundaries and moving on to deeper and richer layers of meaning. Thus when I am moved intuitively, I offer a new understanding or a suggestion that leads to a different kind of expression or experience. Again, the internal frame of reference is the guide. The other person may reject my insight of intuitive discovery, alter it in some way, or embrace it wholeheartedly and move to a new level of understanding.

Rick Copen, after ten years of employing traditional approaches in his work as a psychotherapist, shifted to heuristic psychotherapy with special concentration on intuition as a method of facilitating aware-ness, clarification of issues and personal growth. In an unpublished paper, Copen (1990) describes his use of what he identifies as intuitive connection, defining the process as "an experience in which the therapist and client connect on a very subjective level" (p. 3). Copen illustrates the process in the following example of his therapy work with a young adult:

> T   Can you describe this feeling awful about yourself? What is it like for you when you think you haven't done something perfectly enough.

> Bob moves to the edge of his chair. Again he searches inside—he is silent for several minutes. Then he looks at me and says, "I don't have the words for it."

Now I'm intrigued; something is appearing in his consciousness that he is unable to describe. I move to the edge of my chair. We are sitting closer now, both at the edge of our chairs, almost touching. I want very much to see what is making itself known to Bob. I am aware of our mutual desire to know what Bob is not expressing in words. Bob is still silent, struggling inside to make sense of what he is experiencing, and to verbally share the experience with me. I am there in that place, too, remembering and feeling into the times that I have been unable to articulate my subjective experience.

In this moment with Bob is the origin of the intuitive connection. How it is for him in such a moment of internal struggle with a subjective experience, is just how it is with me in such a moment—the struggle, the frustration, the incapacity in knowing but being unable to identify and express in language. At last I have an idea (which has helped me in the past with my own process).

    T   Suppose you use an analogy to describe your feelings.

He continues to remain silent.

    BOB   (slowly) It's, it's like an explosion inside of me.

We are both still on the edge of our chairs. Bob has previously described the experience of not being good enough. All at once he raises both arms over his head and shakes his head back and forth. His face holds an expression of horror, as if to reveal the terribleness and wrongfulness of not measuring up. I also raise my arms and shake my head back and forth. I too feel the horror of making mistakes, of not being good enough—reminders of my own struggles.

We are looking at each other and suddenly I feel compelled to say, "It's like, oh my God!"

    BOB   Yes! (loudly) That's exactly it, Oh my God! That's how I feel. I have done something awful. Like I have let someone down.
    T   It's like, Oh my God, I've let someone down. Maybe even letting God down (again the intuitive connection).

Bob looked as if he was about to cry. I asked him what he was experiencing.

BOB   Yeah, it's like I have let someone down. (He shakes his head again, looking down.)

T   Tell me more about this "Oh my God" experience. Do you have any memories or feelings attached to this?

BOB   When I was a young child I attended a Catholic school. As a child I always remembered I never wanted to sin.

Bob's face holds a very serious expression now. My image is that of him, but also of me; a little boy struggling always to be good. His being, and mine, revolves around "being good." I feel the intensity and stress of always having to walk the straight line.

In his work with youth and adults, Rick has observed that the intuitive connection consistently enables access to his clients. He states:

Being outside the experience of the client initially, and later being inside on the edge and connecting internally via my own experience, I am able to find the words that give life to the experience. The goal of course, is to help the client get to a place where he or she will describe fully his or her own experience. Intuitive connecting facilitates the sense of mutuality and the client's fuller explication of the damaging subjective experience.

Copen's employment of intuitive connection is closely related to another heuristic concept that I have found applicable in my work: the tacit dimension. In this method, we arrive at knowledge through internal reflection—knowing something without knowing how we know it. It is something we cannot verify or explain or account for; it just is and the therapist presents it. The person in therapy can either accept it or not. The knowledge is tacit, a whole, and cannot be broken into aspects or parts. It must either be received by the other person as a gestalt or cast aside. Underlying every intuition and genuine knowing of any kind is a tacit sense, a hidden dimension, a realization that is prompted by what is known but which requires a tacit connection. The tacit is an ultimate knowledge and, appropriately, can be an effective change agent in heuristic therapy. In my experience, it often is a key to awareness and sometimes makes the major difference in coming to terms with an impossible life.

In this regard, my sessions with Gene, 10 years old, stand out. After many meetings with him in which he described a series of increasingly debilitating illnesses, headaches, nausea, fainting, chronic diarrhea, and insomnia, I stopped listening to his troubles and his angry outbursts. I clearly understood the derivative of his problem: Gene had been responding to everyone but himself for such a long time that he had lost touch with what mattered to him most. He had not, for some while, engaged in his own projects because he was constantly meeting other's needs—his parents, siblings, and teachers, particularly. His body was screaming against this neglect of himself. The illness was a message to get back in touch with himself.

I knew that Gene's recovery depended on recognition of his own creative paths in life. I acted on my tacit knowledge of what was essential, and responded not to his illnesses but to his interests and possibilities for creative expression. Through my comments and questions and mostly through tacit focusing, he came to a new awareness of himself, of what he needed to do to find meaning in his life. I discovered in further talks with him that he had moved completely away from his earlier interest in art, because art was not valued by his achievement-oriented family.

Gene began to experiment with art media in the playroom. It soon became the path to his recovery of energy, excitement, and meaning. His art creations became the center of our world for some time. As he began to experience a sense of self-involvement and fulfillment through art, he was able to include interests that his family shared with him more comfortably. He was able to satisfy others while not neglecting himself. The tacit dimension is a clear indication that, however valuable the explicit plan or goal might be, the unknown mystery will always be a crucial factor in human growth and change.

In utilizing heuristic methods in our relationships, we recognize that subjective knowledge is at the heart of the therapeutic unfolding. One's experience of another person's experience can never be exactly the same as that of the other person, but it can be perceptually congruent. Schutz (1967) has pointed this out: "We may grasp the other's experience with the same perceptual intention that we grasp a thing or event presented to us." When I enter the world of another person, with a heuristic attitude, I come to know that person internally and intimately. My knowing may not be the same as that person's but through our mutual identification of what we have lived before and through empathy the stage is set for rhythmic interchange and feedback. In this process, I perceive what is actually there in the other person's fear, anger, or distress. I also notice what the person has not clearly articulated. In the dialogue that follows, I facilitate the person's fuller understanding in a way that leads to changes in his or her attitudes and behavior.

Rogers (1960) has stated that by reference to the flow of feelings within us we can begin to conceptualize answers to our questions. We can begin to use our energies toward enlightenment and illumination, and thus alter our ways of contacting others. It is just this kind of shift that a heuristic method moves toward in therapy. Tacit knowing accounts for a valid knowledge of a problem, for the therapist's capacity to pursue it, guided by a sense of approaching its solution and utilizing inner sensings and meanings in making judgments and activating new directions.

Through methods of immersion, indwelling, intuition, and the tacit dimension, the therapist arrives at subjective knowledge of the person in therapy and of the relationship. The therapist offers this knowledge; it is either accepted, altered, or rejected. When it is verified, the therapist continues to explore the problem, facilitates the other person's understanding, and eventually grasps its basic constituents. The process of dialogue continues until a mutual position is reached.

In the illumination phase of heuristic therapy, all at once a crucial feeling and/or idea is revealed, an evocation, an epiphany, a light is cast, the dawning of a new meaning. There is now a clearing, a path to explore, meanings to discover. Here is an example from Gayle Beck's (1979) work with a 20-year-college student:

> As John continued to talk about his thoughts on whether or not to continue therapy, I felt like putting my arms around him and rocking him. I knew he was deeply afraid and was unable to verbalize his fears. He began to discuss his inability to be totally honest and open with me and thought this would delay or prevent progress. Suddenly, I knew what his fears were all about! I had the sensation that I was looking inside his head and seeing a movie. John was afraid that I would find out he's "crazy," I would reject him for his "craziness" and he would fall apart. Although I was still feeling sad, the heaviness was lifting and the room seemed lighter and brighter. I let John know that I would be supportive of him in whatever unfolded in our sessions and that I wasn't easily shocked or prone to desert my friends. He gave me a big sigh and I could actually see his muscles begin to untighten and his body become limp. John proceeded to talk about his fantasies. He described scenes of violence against others and himself. A reoccurring fantasy is one where people are beating him with heavy chains and he's enjoying the pain. His self disclosure seemed not to disturb him at that point. I did not experi-

ence fear in him as before. In fact he seemed excited and animated in relating his fantasies. When I asked him to think about his initial reluctance, some of his comments verified my intuitive hunches. He talked about "being different" and being consistently rejected by others for his differences. He confirmed my awareness of his fears of being rejected by me for his craziness.

Thus far, I have elucidated heuristic processes involving methods of entering a person's world, understanding it, delineating the major problems, and finding creative paths for their resolution. Heuristic psychotherapy brings excitement into the challenge of knowing another human being. It involves an active engagement of the therapist as a person and a direct and active engagement between the person in therapy and the therapist. In itself it offers a life-rendering approach, a continual vitality, and a tapping of the resources of the therapist—intellectual, emotional, and spiritual. The energy is alive; the unfolding is dramatic and the depth and meaning experienced bring two human beings into a new sense of what it means to be authentically present and significantly related.

In this sense, heuristic therapy is dialogue and mutuality; it is a series of I-Thou encounters, vividly described by Friedman (1989):

> Genuine dialogue is two-sided, beyond the control of the will. We attain personal wholeness when we respond to the other without thinking of ourselves; and we attain genuine dialogue, not by aiming at it, but by allowing the other to exist in his or her otherness and not just as a content of our experience and thought. We can perceive the other person as whole and unique only through the attitude of a partner and not through that reductive analytical and derivative look that prevails today. (p. 37)

Although dialogue between the partners in psychotherapy is imperative if the heuristic process is to be effective, self-dialogue and self-inquiry are also essential methods. There will be moments during heuristic therapy and between sessions when the therapist will engage in silent internal dialogue—with one's self, one's feelings, or one's understanding as a way of clarifying or finding a direction for therapy—particularly in times when movement is at a standstill. Conversations with one's self will enable the therapist to move back into mutuality at a deeper, more discerning, more meaningful level. The heuristic therapist learns to speak to both sides of an issue as a way of entering into a dialogue that focuses on the polarities or variations in understanding and working through a problem. In self-dialogue, the heuristic therapist may come to think and feel differently, more clearly differentiating the essential constituents, qualities, and dimensions of problems.

Dialogue with the other and dialogue with oneself require active, reflective listening. This means tuning into the other person's communications or one's own and noticing moment by moment what they mean. This kind of discerning reflective listening makes possible the lifting out of previously disguised or unexpressed thoughts and feelings. It enables a shift in self-awareness and self-understanding and often a sense of what action is required to bring a transformation from self-defeat to self-esteem. Barrett-Lennard (1988) describes the process of personal healing and growth that occurs in accurate, receptive listening:

> Sensitive, nonjudgmental, empathic listening, which leads to the experience of being deeply understood, helps to open inner channels and serves as a powerful bridge to others. By being clearly and distinctly heard around some acute but unclear concern, we hear or see ourselves more clearly, and often with less fear. Inner divisions or boundaries tend to dissolve, doors we may have shut on some of our experience begin to open. We may feel freer, more whole, released from some bondage or drain that had been sapping us. We realize we are not alone at the moment of understanding and are freshly aware of what this is like. If this understanding recurs, our sharing can develop a self-propelling quality. (p. 419)

To summarize, there are seven basic phases of the heuristic process. The first involves an *initial engagement* in which a climate of freedom and trust is created and the core theme or problem is determined. The second involves a complete *immersion* in the person's world, going wide open—without prejudice—to know what is, the nature of the problem, its texture, tone, mood, range, and content. This means steeping oneself as a therapist into the other person's world to contact all that is in the other person's communications. This requires full presence to savor, appreciate, touch, feel, and know, without concrete goal or purpose, but through a full immersion, a human presence.

The next phase of the process is that of *incubation*. Once one has come to realize the parameters of the other's world—the components that are critical, in an internal sense—then one mingles freely among them, dwelling inside them in order to arrive at a basic understanding of what is at the core. This is a birth process, the emergence of a significant awareness, of a core theme or themes that will become the focus of therapeutic procedures and interventions.

The next phase of the process is *illumination*. Through observation and timely and appropriate participation, through conversations, dialogues, and self-exploration the texture, detail, and structure of the other's world is revealed. All of its major facets come to be understood. The expanding awareness and deepening meaning enable the person in therapy and the therapist to reach a bond of understanding and knowing that leads to the next step in the process.

From the growing enlightenment, the next phase begins—a full explication of the themes and parameters of the problem. An excerpt of Louise Malefyte's (1976) work with Charles illustrates the process of explication:

T   You'd like your mom to understand you better . . . understand kids better . . . rather than just say . . . all you do is party . . .

C   Yeah, that was back before . . . it all was brought up today . . . like the cycle that I went through . . . like the partying and how I related to other people . . . made them sort of isolated to that certain attitude of kids . . . you know . . . an isolated attitude . . . it isolated them to look at me in only that way . . . which, made a blockade . . . like . . . I couldn't, I couldn't find a way out of it . . .

T   They saw you in only one way . . .

C   Right.

T   And you were stuck in that one way . . .

C   Right . . . and this took place in school, with other people.

T   Teachers saw you in that one way, other people . . .

C   Right, yeah, right (laughing-crying sounds) . . . it was like, when is he going to change . . . when is he going to come out of this . . . it's like I've come to my senses . . . you know, really, I was intelligent . . . and for a long time I didn't understand that . . . what's wrong with me . . . what's going on . . . given a little bit . . . a little respect and a little love I'd, ah, do anything . . .

T   What do you mean . . . given a little respect . . . and given a little love . . .

C   You know, they was always looking at me . . . like, when is he going to change . . . and that was what was making me like that . . . in a way . . . and a lot of it was myself, too . . . if it was just all turned around and everyone looked at everyone in the right way . . . I know that's impossible . . . if they did, it would help people out, you know . . .

T   If they had looked at you and seen that there was more to you.

C   Right.

T   Than this kid who wasn't coming to school, who was high all the time . . .

C   In other words, they condemned me all the time.

T   As someone who spent most of his time partying.

C   Getting in trouble and spending most of my time in the office.

T   And if they saw you, and if they looked for you and said Charles, maybe you're hurting somewhere.

C   Right . . . and they didn't say nothing 'bout hurting . . . they didn't say that I was hurting myself . . . that I was looking at . . . or not looking at this . . . they didn't tell me nothin' . . . they sort of like shied away.

T   That really hurt . . . that really hurt . . .

C   Just looking at people and they wasn't big enough to come up to me . . . and tell me what was my problem . . .

T   Come up to you and say, you're doing yourself in . . .

C   And that would have made me feel great . . . feel great . . . so . . . that was my problem for a long time . . . and now . . . I still sort of have the problem . . . people are still . . . er . . . afraid of me . . . they look upon me . . . more than I am, sort of, right now . . . I mean they, well . . .

T   They think of you as a super person.

C   Well, no . . . they just see more . . . they see more in me, so then they expect more of me . . . than I'm capable of doing . . .

T   So you're still not being touched as a real live person . . .

C   And, and, and I look, and what's the deal here . . . one time you're looking at me with anger . . . and then, no one tells me shit, I mean, you know . . . how am I supposed to turn around without knowing nothin' . . . so I have to sort of irritate and butt in and find out what's going on . . . and then people turn away . . . because they think you're stupid . . . I'm supposed to be enjoying myself . . . and I have to find out some things . . . boy, that bugs me, ya know, like at home . . . it's sort of the same way . . . how would you feel if you got lots of questions asked or people to ask you questions . . . without answers . . . to your own questions and to bring them out . . . and somebody's telling you, you know . . . that you should start giving . . . and talking . . . that is . . . sort of true . . . that irritates . . . that hurts . . .

T   What would you like to say to your mother . . . which you don't dare . . .

C   She was right though . . . she was right . . . what I'd like to say to her would have been something like calming her down . . . tell her she was right . . . and, ah, let's start working together . . . and doing some things, ah, you know . . . get stuff accomplished . . . I don't know . . . that just makes me feel good, ya know . . . the same old people, ya know . . . my mom, my brother . . . my dad's moving out . . . I mean . . . that's all part of life . . . ya know . . . I want to change that into a different style . . .

T   What's this other style . . . how'd you like to change it?

C   It's like (hesitating) they expect so much of me . . . but can't come up to me and say it . . . there's, there's girls in the school . . . I had been watching . . . and looking . . . and looking like they'd like me to say something . . . ya know . . . without . . .

T   Encouragement.

C   And then they . . . they don't know how to go about it . . . I mean, they want me to say something and then they don't look at me . . . I need a little petting-up . . . which they know I do . . .

T   You're wanting somebody to say I like you . . .

C   That's part . . . yeah . . . part one of it.

T   It's like you don't have enough strokes . . . you want more . . .

C   Right, I don't know . . . I don't know . . . I feel useless, like, they're just caving in on me and giving up . . . there's nothing there, nothing . . .

T   What would you like to do?

C   (laughs) Be creative, uh, make them feel loved, soothing, and, uh . . . ya know . . . stuff like that . . .

T   Maybe hold somebody's hands . . .

C   If people came up to me . . . and, you know . . . like you're doing right now . . . sort of encouraging . . . and that would make me feel stronger . . . I'll bet you that my face would just light right up . . .

In the explication phase, presented in the above example, Charles and his therapist focused on the problem of rejection as Charles was perceiving it. The therapist's presence and her comments enabled him to explicate his initial statement of the problem that his mother did not understand him enough. The clarification brought in his teachers, who also did not understand him, and his peers who expected too much of him. Being understood was the initial focus, but as this emphasis was explored there was the realization that being expected to be different and to change was more disturbing and hurtful. There was also the understanding that not being understood and being expected to change evoked both sadness and anger.

Getting into trouble in school and spending considerable time in the office was Charles' way of getting attention as well as his way of protest, but it was also experienced by him as not satisfying. He wanted to be recognized, seen, and encouraged to take responsibility for the troubles he brought on himself. In the explication process, he recognized that what he needed was "a little petting-up," more strokes, "a little respect," and "a little love". Thus ultimately the problem was not being accepted and not being challenged to be responsible. To begin to shift he recognized the need for positive attention and love.

Throughout the explication phase, the heuristic therapist utilizes a focusing method similar to that developed by Gendlin (1978). Gendlin's steps include:

(1) *Clearing a space.* Be silent, just to yourself.
(2) *Felt sense.* From among what comes, select one problem. Do not go inside it. Stand back from it.
(3) *Handle.* What is the quality of this unclear felt sense? Let a word, phrase or image come up.
(4) *Resonating.* Go back and forth between the felt sense and the word. See if a bodily signal tells you they fit; capture the quality of the felt sense.
(5) *Asking.* What is it about this whole problem that makes this quality? Touch it, tap it, be with it. Be with the felt sense until something comes along with it, a shift, a slight "give" or release.
(6) *Receive.* Receive whatever comes with a shift in a friendly way. Stay with it for a few moments. If you have sensed and touched an unclear holistic body sense of this problem, then you have focused in a friendly way.

During the explication phase, the primary constituents of the person's world are delineated and explored. When the explication is complete, the therapist is challenged to portray the situation as a whole to develop a creative synthesis. This comes through reflection and dialogue with the person in therapy as more and more of the pieces fit into a total picture. The creative synthesis brings together the relevant factors of ambition, hope, expectancy, distortion, and denial and points the way to a new vision and plan of action.

The creative synthesis is the unified picture of the person in his or her world. All the parts fit together in an integrated way, forming an integral theme or world view that enables one to understand how this person sees himself or herself and his or her life. The external situation may remain the same, but an internal bodily shift has occurred. The person has moved from a self-defeating view of his or her place in the world to a sense of being competent to meet life's challenges, with an uplift of self-confidence and self-esteem that casts new light on both identity and destiny.

Doris, for example, in a creative synthesis realized that she had internalized her supervisor's view of her. Since her years in the convent, she almost automatically internalized the voices of authority. These voices were everywhere and dominated her life. She translated the voices into a symphonic poem, with the same refrain appearing again and again. An internal bodily shift occurred. Now she could distinguish her employer's words from her own; his evaluations no longer affected her judgment of herself. Her song was the creative synthesis.

When she put it into action, Doris was carrying out the last phase of the heuristic process—the course of action. In doing so, Doris deliberately and consciously no longer considered her employer's directives as representing the truth. Her own judgment of her performance was something she came to respect. In time, the words he directed to her changed. She was standing her ground, pointing to her productivity, and using a language that reflected a valuing of herself. It rubbed off on him and his assessments of her work performance became much more positive. During the action phase, Doris had the support and encouragement of her therapist. Her knowledge shift, insight shift, and bodily shift changed her self-concept and the meaning of her work life. Her employer's external frame of reference no longer controlled her. Her frame of reference in time affected him and brought him to the realization that he could no longer dismiss her or the effectiveness of her work, decisions, and actions. The course of action is the challenge to put into practice the illumination and explication of the facets of the problem and the underlying structures that account for it.

The work of heuristic therapy or research reaches its pinnacle in taking into life active self-awarenesses, insights, and clarifications. As Polanyi (1962) has pointed out, "Heuristic passion is . . . the mainspring of originality—the force which impels us to abandon an accepted framework of interpretation and commit ourselves, by the crossing of a logical gap, to the use of a new framework" (p. 159). The lifting out of the full nature, essence, and meaning of the experience brings one into touch with creative resources, enables one to develop a new view of self and life, and makes possible movement toward authenticity, self-efficacy, and well-being.

NOTE

1. The section on loneliness is a revision of material published in *Individuality and Encounter* (Moustakas, 1968) and *The Touch of Loneliness* (Moustakas, 1975).

References

Barrett-Lennard, G. T. (1988). Listening. *Person-Centered Review, 3*(4), 410-425.

Barrineau, P., & Bozarth, J. D. (1989). A person-centered research model. *Person-Centered Review. 4*(4), 465-474.

Beck, G. (1979). *Heuristic psychotherapy.* Unpublished paper. Detroit, MI: Merrill-Palmer Institute.

Benyei, C. R. (1988). *Mother.* Unpublished poem, Union Institute, Cincinnati.

Bernthal, N. (1990). *Motherhood lost and found: The experience of becoming an adoptive mother to a foreign born child.* Unpublished doctoral dissertation, Union Institute, Cincinnati.

Blau, D. (1980). Through the eyes of the beholder: A phenomenological study of anger. (Doctoral dissertation, Humanistic Psychology Institute, 1980). *Dissertation Abstracts International, 41,* 681B.

Bridgman, P. (1950). *Reflections of a physicist.* New York: Philosophical Library.

Bronowski, J. (1965). *Science and human values.* New York: Harper & Row.

Buber, M. (1958). *I and thou.* New York: Scribners.

Buber, M. (1961). *Tales of the Hasidim: The early masters* (O. Marx, Trans.). New York: Schocken.

Buber, M. (1965). *The knowledge of man.* New York: Harper & Row.

Buhl, H. (1956). *Lonely challenge.* (H. Merrick, Trans.). New York: Dutton.

Burgess, P. (1940). *Who walk alone.* New York: Holt, Rinehart and Winston.

Byrd, R. E. (1938). *Alone.* New York: G. P. Putnam's Sons.

Capra, F. (1982). *The turning point.* New York: Simon & Schuster.

Chambers, W. (1952). *Witness.* New York: Random House.

Chase, R. (1951). *Emily Dickinson.* New York: William Sloan Associates.

Cheyne, V. (1989). Growing up in a fatherless home: The female experience. (Doctoral dissertation, Union for Experimenting Colleges and Universities, 1988). *Dissertation Abstracts International, 49,* 5558-B.

Clark, J. (1988). Duet: The experience of the psychologically androgynous male. (Doctoral dissertation, Union for Experimenting Colleges and Universities, 1987). *Dissertation Abstracts International, 49,* 235-B.

Combs, A., Richards, A., & Richards, F. (1976). *Perceptual psychology.* New York: Harper & Row.

Copen, R. (1990). *Intuitive connecting.* Unpublished paper. Detroit, MI: The Center for Humanistic Studies.

Coulson, W., & Rogers, C. (Eds.). (1968). *Man and the science of man.* Columbus, OH: Merrill.

Craig, E. (1978). The heart of the teacher: A heuristic study of the inner world of teaching. (Doctoral dissertation, Boston University, 1978). *Dissertation Abstracts International, 38,* 7222A.

Day, D. (Ed.). (1952). *Woodrow Wilson's own story.* Boston: Little, Brown.

Descartes, R. (1977). *The essential writings* (J. J. Blom, Trans.). New York: Harper & Row.

Dickinson, E. (1927). *The complete poems of Emily Dickinson,* Boston, MA: Little, Brown.

Douglass, B., & Moustakas, C. (1985). Heuristic inquiry: The internal search to know. *Journal of Humanistic Psychology. 25*(3), 39-55.

Feild, R. (1976). *The invisible way.* New York: Harper & Row.

Frick, W. (1983). The symbolic growth experience. *Journal of Humanistic Psychology, 23,* 108-125.

Frick, W. B. (1987a). The symbolic growth experience and the creation of meaning. *International Forum for Logotherapy, 10,* 35-40.

Frick, W. B. (1987b). The symbolic growth experience: Paradigm for a humanistic-existential learning theory. *Journal of Humanistic Psychology, 27,* 406-423.

Frick, W. B. (1990). The symbolic growth experience: A chronicle of heuristic inquiry and a quest for synthesis. *Journal of Humanistic Psychology, 30,* 64-80.

Friedman, M. (1989). Dialogue, confirmation, and the image of the human. *ICIS Forum, 19*(1), 36-42.

Fromm, E. (1941). *Escape from freedom.* New York: Holt, Rinehart and Winston.

Fromm-Reichmann, F. (1959). Loneliness, *Psychiatry, 22,* 1-16.

Gendlin, E. (1962). *Experiencing and the creation of meaning.* Chicago: Free Press.

Gendlin, E. (1978). *Focusing.* New York: Everest House.

Hawka, S. (1986). The experience of feeling unconditionally loved. (Doctoral dissertation, Union for Experimenting Colleges and Universities, 1985). *Dissertation Abstracts International, 46,* 4385-B.

Herndon, W., & Weik, J. W. (1920). *Abraham Lincoln* (Vol. I and II). New York: Appleton-Century-Crofts.

Hiss, A. (1957). *In the court of public opinion.* New York: Knopf.

Humphrey, E. (1989). *Searching for meaning.* Unpublished doctoral dissertation, Union Institute, Cincinnati.

Jourard, S. (1968). *Disclosing man to himself.* New York: Van Nostrand.

Jourard, S. (1971). *Self-disclosure: An experimental analysis of the transparent self.* New York: Wiley-Interscience.

Kant, I. (1929). *Critique of pure reason* (N. K. Smith, Ed.). New York: St. Martin Press.

Keen, E. (1975). *A primer on phenomenological psychology.* New York: Holt, Rinehart & Winston.

Kelly, G. A. (1969). Humanistic methodology in psychological research. *Journal of Humanistic Psychology, 11*(1), 53-65.

Kierkegaard, S. (1941). *Concluding unscientific postscript* (D. F. Swenson, Trans.). Princeton, NJ: Princeton University Press.

Kierkegaard, S. (1965). *The point of view for my work as an author* (B. Nelson, Ed.). New York: Harper & Row.

Kuhn, T. (1970). *The structure of scientific revolutions.* Chicago, IL: University of Chicago Press.

Lusseyran, J. (1987). *And there was light.* New York: Parabola.

MacIntyre, M. (1983). The experience of shyness. (Doctoral dissertation, Saybrook Institute, 1982). *Dissertation Abstracts International, 43,* 3016-B.

Malefyte, L. (1976). *The explication process in heuristic psychotherapy.* Unpublished manuscript. Detroit, MI: Merrill-Palmer Institute.

Marshall, R. (1987). A journey through non-causal dimensions: A heuristic study of synchronicity. (Doctoral dissertation, Union for Experimenting Colleges and Universities, 1987). *Dissertation Abstracts International, 48,* 2125-B.

Maslow, A. (1956). Self-actualizing people: A study of psychological health. In Moustakas (Ed.), *The self* (pp. 160-194). New York: Harper & Brothers.

Maslow, A. H. (1966). *The psychology of science*. New York: Harper & Row.

Maslow, A. (1971). *The farther reaches of human nature*. New York: Viking.

McNally, C. (1982). The experience of being sensitive. (Doctoral dissertation, Union Graduate School, 1982). *Dissertation Abstracts International, 43*, 4156-B.

Menninger, K. (1942). *Love against hate*. New York: Harcourt, Brace and World.

Moffitt, J. (1971). To look at any thing. In *Since feeling is first* (p. 149). J. Mecklenberger & G. Simmons (Eds.), Glenview, IL: Scott, Foresman.

Moore, G. E. (1959). *Principia ethica*. New York: Cambridge University Press.

Moustakas, C. (1961). *Loneliness*. Englewood Cliffs, NJ: Prentice-Hall.

Moustakas, C. (1967). Heuristic research. In J. F. T. Bugental (Ed.), *Challenges of humanistic psychology*. New York: McGraw-Hill.

Moustakas, C. (1968). *Individuality and encounter*. Cambridge, MA: Doyle.

Moustakas, C. (1972). *Loneliness and love*. Englewood Cliffs, NJ: Prentice-Hall.

Moustakas, C. (1975). *The touch of loneliness*. Englewood Cliffs, NJ: Prentice-Hall.

Moustakas, C. (1981). *Rhythms, rituals, and relationships*. Detroit: Center for Humanistic Studies.

Moustakas, C. (1988). *Phenomenology, science, and psychotherapy*. Sydney, Nova Scotia: Family Life Institute, University College of Cape Breton.

O'Hara, M. (1986). Heuristic inquiry as psychotherapy. *Person-Centered Review, 1*(2). 172-184.

Patton, M. (1980). *Qualitative evaluation methods*. Beverly Hills, CA: Sage.

Patton, M. (1986). *Utilization-focused evaluation*. Beverly Hills, CA: Sage.

Patton, M. Q. (1990). Humanistic psychology and humanistic research. *Person-Centered Review, 5* (2), 191-202.

Pearce, J. C. (1971). *The crack in the cosmic egg*. New York: Julian.

Polanyi, M. (1962). *Personal knowledge*. Chicago: University of Chicago Press.

Polanyi, M. (1964). *Science, faith and society*. Chicago: University of Chicago Press.

Polanyi, M. (1966). *The tacit dimension*. Garden City, NY: Doubleday.

Polanyi, M. (1969). *Knowing and being* (Marjorie Grene, Ed.). Chicago: University of Chicago Press.

Polanyi, M. (1983). *The tacit dimension*. Gloucester, MA: Peter Smith.

Potts, M. (1988). *The meaning of the precognitive dream experience*. Unpublished doctoral dissertation, Union Institute, Cincinnati.

Prefontaine, C. (1979). Transforming self-doubt into self-confidence. (Doctoral dissertation, Humanistics Psychology Institute). *Dissertation Abstracts International, 41*, 170-A.

Riesman, D., Denny, R., & Glazer, N. (1950). *The lonely crowd*. New Haven, CT: Yale University Press.

Roads, M. (1987). *Talking with nature*. Tiburn, CA: H. J. Kramer.

Robertson, J. (1959). *Young children in hospitals*. New York: Basic Books.

Rodriguez, A. (1985). A heuristic-phenomenological investigation of Mexican American ethnic identity. (Doctoral dissertation, Union for Experimenting Colleges and Universities, 1984). *Dissertation Abstracts International, 46*, 313-B.

Rogers, C. R. (1951). *Client-centered therapy*. Boston: MA: Houghton-Mifflin.

Rogers, C. R. (1957). The necessary and sufficient conditions of therapeutic personality change. *Journal of Consulting Psychology, 21*(2), 95-103.

Rogers, C. R. (1960). Toward a science of the person. In T. Sutich and M. Vick (Eds.), *Readings in humanistic psychology*. New York: Free Press.

Rogers, C. R. (1965). Some thoughts regarding the current philosophy of the behavioral sciences. *Journal of Humanistic Psychology, 5*, 182-194.

Rogers, C. R. (1968). Some thoughts regarding the current assumptions of the behavioral sciences. In W. Coulson and C. R. Rogers (Eds.), *Man and the science of man*. Columbus, OH: Merrill.

Rogers, C. R. (1969). Toward a science of the person. In *Readings in humanistic psychology* (A. J. Sutich & M. A. Vick, Eds.). New York: Macmillan.

Rogers, C. (1985). Toward a more human science of the person. *Journal of Humanistic Psychology, 25*(4), 7-24.

Rogers, C. R. (1989). *Carl Rogers: Dialogues* (H. Kirschenbaum & V. L. Henderson, Eds.). Boston, MA: Houghton Mifflin.

Rourke, P. (1984). The experience of being inspired. (Doctoral dissertation, Saybrook Institute, 1983). *Dissertation Abstracts International, 45*, 1296-B.

Saint-Exupery, A. (1939). *Wind, sand, and stars*. (L. Galantiere, Trans.). New York: Reynal & Hitchcock.

Saint-Exupery, A. (1957). *Night flight*. (S. Gilbert, Trans.). New York: Appleton-Century-Crofts.

Salk, J. (1983). *Anatomy of reality*. New York: Columbia University Press.

Schopenhauer, A. (1966). *The world as will and representation* (E. F. J. Payne, Trans.). New York: Doves.

Schultz, D. (1983). The experience of self-reclamation of former Catholic religious women. (Doctoral dissertation, Saybrook Institute, 1983). *Dissertation Abstracts International, 44*, 926-B.

Schutz, A. (1967). *The phenomenology of the social world*. Evanston, IL: Northwestern University Press.

Shaw, R. (1989). *The heartbeat of relationships: A heuristic investigation of interaction rhythms*. Unpublished doctoral dissertation, Union Institute, Cincinnati.

Snyder, J. (1983). *The initial interview in heuristic psychotherapy*. Unpublished manuscript. Detroit, MI: The Center for Humanistic Studies.

Snyder, J. (1989). The experience of really feeling connected to nature. (Doctoral dissertation, Union for Experimenting Colleges and Universities, 1988). *Dissertation Abstracts International, 49*, 4025-B.

Snyder, R. (1988). *The experience of rejecting love*. Unpublished doctoral dissertation, Union Institute, Cincinnati.

Spivack, L. (1985). *An ode to my mom*. Unpublished poem, Union Institute, Cincinnati.

Steinbeck, J., & Ricketts, E. F. (1941). *Sea of Cortez*. New York: Viking Press.

Sullivan, H. S. (1953). *The interpersonal theory of psychiatry*. New York: Norton.

Tabor, E. (1950). *The cliff's edge: Songs of a psychotic*. New York: Sheed & Ward.

Thoreau, H. D. (1955). *Walden and other writings* (B. Atkinson, Ed.). New York: Random House.

van Dusen, W. (1973). The presence of spirits in madness. In J. Fademan & D. Kewman (Eds.), *Exploring madness: Experience, theory and research* (pp. 118-134). Monterey, CA: Brooks/Cole.

Varani, J. (1985). Psychological dimensions of mystery: A phenomenological-heuristic investigation. (Doctoral dissertation, Union for Experimenting Colleges and Universities, 1984). *Dissertation Abstracts International, 45*, 3349-B.

Vaughn, L. (1989). *The experience of writing poetry.* Unpublished doctoral dissertation, Union Institute, Cincinnati.

Weber, S. J. (1986). The nature of interviewing. *Phenomenology and Pedagogy,* 4(2), 65-72.

Wolfe, T. (1941). *The hills beyond.* New York: Harper & Row.

Wood, M. (1953). *Paths of loneliness.* New York: Columbia University Press.

About the Author

CLARK MOUSTAKAS, Ph.D., Ed.D., is President of the Center for Humanistic Studies in Detroit and Senior Consultant and Core Faculty member in psychology at the Union Institute in Cincinnati. His development as a person and as a psychologist is reflected in his studies and publications grounded in psychological, philosophic, educational, and literary perspectives, values, and concepts that underlie, enrich, and deepen human discoveries, meanings, and experiences. His publications on loneliness, creativity and conformity, teaching and learning, psychotherapy, and qualitative research retain an interdisciplinary and humanities unity of mind and soul.